Trains to Nowhere:

British Steam Train Accidents 1906–1960

'Steam Past' Books from Allen & Unwin

THE LIMITED by O. S. Nock
THE BIRTH OF BRITISH RAIL by Michael R. Bonavia
STEAM'S INDIAN SUMMER by George Heiron & Eric Treacy
GRAVEYARD OF STEAM by Brian Handley
PRESERVED STEAM IN BRITAIN by Patrick B. Whitehouse
MEN OF THE GREAT WESTERN by Peter Grafton
TRAVELLING BY TRAIN IN THE EDWARDIAN AGE by Philip Unwin
MAUNSELL'S NELSONS by D. W. Winkworth
MAN OF THE SOUTHERN: JIM EVANS LOOKS BACK by Jim Evans
STEAM, a year book edited by Roger Crombleholme and Terry Kirtland

Trains to Nowhere

British Steam Train Accidents 1906–1960

J. A. B. Hamilton

Second edition revised by Malcolm Gerard

London
GEORGE ALLEN & UNWIN
Boston Sydney

First published in 1967 as *British Railway Accidents of the Twentieth Century*

Second edition, revised and re-set 1981
Second impression 1982

GEORGE ALLEN & UNWIN LTD
40 Museum Street, London WC1A 1LU

© George Allen & Unwin (Publishers) Ltd, 1967, 1981

British Library Cataloguing in Publication Data

Hamilton, J. A. B.
   Trains to nowhere. – 2nd ed.
   1. Railroads – Great Britain – Accidents
   I. Title
   625.1   HE1783.G7   80-42233

   ISBN 0–04–385084–7

Picture editor: Mike Esau

Set in 10 on 12 point Bembo by Nene Phototypesetters Ltd
and printed in Great Britain by
Biddles Ltd, Guildford, Surrey.

Contents

Illustrations

Photographs

Figures

Preface

The distinguished railway author, J. A. B. Hamilton, died in 1971. In the mid 1960s he wrote 'British Railway Accidents of the Twentieth Century' as he felt there was a gap in the available literature on the subject. L. T. C. Rolt's 'Red For Danger' was, and is, the standard work on such accidents in their relation to the development of safety measures, and contains a comprehensive review of that aspect. But Mr Hamilton wanted to go into more detail on some of the disasters and was particularly interested in the human side of the subject. Since, however, he abhorred sensationalism, most of the more harrowing details are not included. He drew largely on the official reports and contemporary sources for his material, visiting the locations where possible. To this he added his own life-long experience and love of railways, imparting the book with a special quality of his own.

In adapting his work for the 'Steam Past' series, I have endeavoured to retain as much as I could of the flavour of the original edition. Since it was necessary to reduce the total length by about half, this has perhaps not always been completely possible, and I hope I will be forgiven if occasionally I may not have wholly succeeded. I have, however, added a chapter on Settle since this proved to be the last major disaster involving working steam. To help the reader follow events leading to some of the accidents I have also prepared six new diagrams.

In his foreword to the original book, Mr Hamilton made the following acknowledgements: 'Grateful thanks to L. T. C. Rolt for the use of material from "Red For Danger" and to Hamilton Ellis and his publishers for permission to use part of "The Trains We Loved" in the Salisbury sequence. Thanks also to J. G. Holmes for permission to draw on his Quintinshill article published in *Railway World*.' Lastly he thanked all the many railway employees who had helped him in his research.

M. GERARD
October 1980

I
The Midnight Runaways

SALISBURY (London and South Western Railway)
GRANTHAM (Great Northern Railway)
SHREWSBURY (London and North Western Railway)

Three times in just over a year, a train sped to destruction on a curve at night by a station. It happened first at Salisbury just before two in the morning of Sunday 1 July 1906.

Before Southampton became an ocean port, the American Line ships used to call each week at Plymouth to offload mails and such passengers as were anxious to reach London quickly. The Great Western had secured the mails, possibly because of useful connections at Bristol, but the South Western lured the passengers with its sixteen-mile shorter route, although this advantage was lost on the very day of the accident.

On the evening of 30 June the liner, 'New York', landed forty-three passengers at Stonehouse Pool. The boat train, a modest five-vehicle affair with T9 class no. 288 in front, left Devonport at 11 pm on its four hours twenty minutes schedule to Waterloo. At Templecombe, nearly halfway up the line to London, Driver Robins and Fireman Gadd were waiting to take the train forward. Robins was young for his position, only forty, and this was his first trip with the boat special. His engine was not another T9 but one of the newer and larger L12 class, no. 421, with boiler-centre pitched nine inches higher.

No. 288 had made a good run from Devonport and no. 421 was able to set out punctually on the remaining 112 mile run to London, scheduled in 116 minutes. The night inspector and a shunter had spoken to the engine crew and could testify afterwards that both were sober and in good spirits.

Robins made no attempt to hurry at the start and by Dinton, twenty miles out, he had dropped four minutes. Down the long falling gradients to Salisbury the speed rose to something over 70 mph – by no means exceptional for this stretch. But at the approach to Salisbury he merely shut off steam and neglected to apply the brake, despite the 30 mph limit for the curves on either side of the station. No. 421 negotiated the west curve with the whistle screaming, dashed headlong through the station and miraculously kept the rails over the 7½-chain reverse curve beyond. But on the succeeding 10-chain curve the enormous centrifugal force took effect. Helped by a 3½-inch cant the engine was not derailed, but on the left-hand curve it heeled over to the right and the left-side wheels lifted from the rails. Even so it might have righted itself, but by evil chance a train of milk empties was passing on the down line. No. 421 struck the vans as it canted over, then overbalanced completely as it flew off at a tangent, crashed into a Beyer Peacock goods engine that was standing in the Bournemouth bay and came to rest on its side across the down track. The tender folded up on the engine, and the carriages piled up in a heap of wreckage against the tender and the parapet of the Fisherton Street Bridge. The first three vehicles were destroyed and the fourth had its side torn off; only the kitchen-brake at the rear escaped serious damage. Five vans of the milk train were also destroyed. The only horror that was not added was fire. It started, but was quickly extinguished by jets from the town hydrants.

Twenty-four passengers lost their lives in the accident and none of the remainder escaped injury. The driver and fireman were crushed between engine and tender and their bodies were recovered horribly mutilated. The guard of the milk train was also killed and the fireman of the goods engine died from his injuries. Its driver was badly scalded by escaping steam.

Why did Driver Robins speed to his destruction? The Inspecting Officer, Major Pringle, found his recklessness inexplicable. The Inspector recommended that the 30 mph restriction round the east curves should be reduced to 15 – a recommendation which had no bearing on the cause of the accident. More to the point was a suggestion that the distant signals at Salisbury

1. Salisbury. A view of the clearing-up operations looking towards London across the Fisherton Street Bridge. The eight-wheeled 'Watercart' tender of the L12 can be clearly seen in the middle of the wreckage, whilst the top of the chimney of the Beyer Peacock goods locomotive is just visible in front of the telegraph pole at the far end of the carriage top. (*Illustrated London News*)

should be kept at danger, to remind drivers of the restriction.

The Company solved the problem another way. Immediately after the accident the Templecombe stop was abolished; the boat trains changed engines at Exeter and Salisbury just like the ordinary expresses, and fourteen minutes were added to the schedule.

As always after a mysterious disaster, rumours started, particularly as on the same day the Great Western had opened its direct route via Castle Cary and put an end to the South Western's distance advantage. This was enough to start the story that Robins had been tipped off to 'show 'em', but remarks he made at Templecombe and his leisurely start firmly discount this. Nor, as some believed at the time, could it be supposed that he had mistaken his whereabouts. His whistling as he approached the station showed that he was alert and knew exactly where he was.

It seems that this adds up to a perfectly rational explanation: Robins simply did not realise the risk he was running. He had never passed through Salisbury without stopping before, so that he had no experience of a severe restriction in the middle of a high-speed stretch. Maybe too he had heard stories of other drivers' speed exploits with the T9s. But that extra nine inches in the centre of gravity caused him to overdo it – just. Only just, because it was calculated

2. Salisbury. The Beyer Peacock engine has been removed but its tender is still in position. The damaged L12 4–4–0 no. 421 is being hoisted out of the remains of the leading coach. (*Illustrated London News*)

3. Grantham. An artist's impression of the scene at sunrise. (*Illustrated London News*)

afterwards that to cause the engine to overturn on that curve would require a speed of at least 67 mph.

Or was this an error of judgement on the part of a tired man? Robins had been on duty for nine and a half hours at the time of the accident and would have had to continue for at least a couple of hours more. Such was the railwayman's lot in the railways' heyday.

If there was a reasonable explanation at Salisbury, there was none at Grantham less than three months later. On the night of 19 September 1906, the East Coast Mail, which had left King's Cross at 8.45 pm and was due to stop at Grantham, ran through the station at speed and was derailed at the far end where the points were set for the curve onto the Nottingham branch. How an experienced driver, who knew the road intimately and had worked this same turn the night before, could go careering to destruction in this fashion was a mystery which sorely perplexed our forefathers. The Moorgate Tube disaster in 1975 was to pose a similar puzzle for the present generation.

Though only a small country town, Grantham was the Great Northern's principal staging point on its route to the North. Most expresses stopped there and nearly all those that did so changed engines. The 8.45 was an exception; it formed the last leg of a Doncaster–York–Peterborough–Doncaster turn. Nevertheless the habit of engine-changing almost certainly had a bearing on the accident.

As the diagram shows, to reach the loco sheds

12

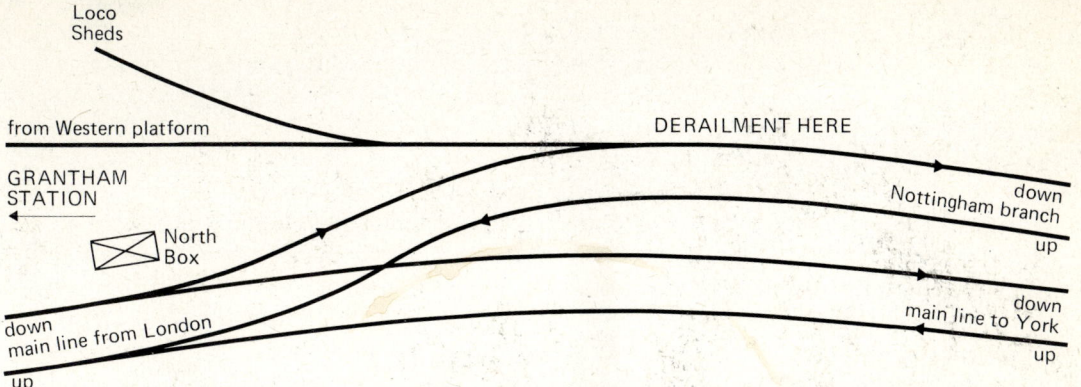

Figure 1. Grantham: track layout

– now demolished – required a run up the branch and a back shunt into the engine yard. It was the custom, therefore, when an express stopped, to have the points ready set for the off-going engine to run onto the branch.

The 8.45 was first and foremost a mail and parcels train; its arrival times in the North were hardly such as to attract many passengers. On this night, of its twelve-coach load only five were passenger vehicles, including two sleeping-cars, occupied by no more than about fifty travellers. It was indeed fortunate that the train was not better filled.

Awaiting the Mail at Peterborough was no. 276, one of the Ivatt large-boilered Atlantics, at that time only two years old. Driver Fleetwood on the footplate had had charge of her ever since she was built – one engine, one driver was still the rule. His regular fireman was off sick but deputising was a very competent young man named Talbot, who had been a premium apprentice at Doncaster and was now gaining road experience. A capable pair, and railway staff who spoke to them at Peterborough could testify that both were sober and in every way normal.

At Grantham it was nearly eleven o'clock, the time when the Mail was due. It was a dark night but perfectly clear despite the occasional rain which had made the rails greasy. Signalman Day in the South box was the first official at Grantham to see the train which he accepted from Saltersford at 11.01. No. 276 should have whistled as she approached the station but on this night there was no whistle. The next thing Day saw was that the train was passing his box, not at a moderate speed in readiness for the stop, but at something like 50 mph. The surprised signalman just had time to catch a glimpse of the men on the footplate – the only man at Grantham to do so – and could say afterwards that both appeared to be standing motionless, one on either side, each looking through his spectacle glass.

Guard Knighton, the front guard of the express, had noticed that his train had not slowed down. As he passed the South box he opened his window and found the train still travelling, as he put it, at a terrific pace. He seized the brake handle, but there was no vacuum. It would seem that the driver had applied the brakes only the moment before.

On the platform were a few intending passengers and a group of postmen waiting to load the mails. They saw the lights of the approaching locomotive nearing them a great deal faster

13

than they should, so fast, according to one of the passengers, that the current of air swept parcels off a barrow on the platform. One of the postmen noticed sparks coming from the wheels as if the brakes had been applied. So far as he could observe in a fleeting moment, steam had been shut off. Other observers would be found to say that the brakes had not been applied, and the engine was too badly damaged for the brake handle to supply the answer.

At the other end of the station in the North box, Signalman Scoffin had just passed a goods from Leicester, coming down from the Nottingham branch, onto the up main line, and set the down points for the branch – as a safety precaution it was explained afterwards. If so, it was an unnecessary one, as the goods was fully protected by the signals. Having set the points thus Scoffin left them there; this it was stated at the inquiry was in accordance with the regulations. To Scoffin's amazement no. 276 ran past his box at a speed which he estimated to be at least 40 mph, although he thought that the train was sliding along the rails as if skidding due to the application of the brakes.

A few moments of horrified silence, then a noise like an explosion and a sheet of flame lit the night sky to the north of the station. The Atlantic, with its short fixed wheelbase, had

4. Grantham. A newspaper photograph of the wreckage at the foot of the embankment after the fire had been extinguished. (*Illustrated London News*)

5. Shrewsbury. Experiment class no. 2052, 'Stephenson', lying where it ended its disastrous journey with the mangled remains of most of its complement of carriages heaped up behind. The impression of the coach on top is that it was made from rather inferior matchwood. Note the tender devoid of coal. (*Radio Times Hulton Picture Library*)

ridden the reverse curve onto the branch, but the tender had become derailed and swept away the parapet of the Harlaxton Road underbridge. It then broke away and plunged down the thirty-foot embankment. In doing so it derailed the engine, which slewed broadside across the tracks. The front three vehicles, mercifully all vans, piled up against the engine; the next six followed the tender down the embankment, and only the last three remained on the rails undamaged. Fire broke out in the wreckage both above and below, caused above by coals from the engine and below by escaping gas, but there are no records of any charred bodies. The driver and fireman were killed instantly; eleven of the modest complement of passengers died as well as a postal sorter.

Why? If the points had been set for the main line the express would have continued harmlessly on its way until sooner or later it was brought to a standstill. Yet this so-called safety measure steered it to its destruction. There is no proof, but the safety claim made by the Superintendent of the Running Department was probably no more than a cover-up for a slightly risky method of working, which as I have explained was to set the points for the Nottingham branch ready for the off-coming engine. It was risky because any driver who misjudged his stop – and such things have been known to happen, especially on a falling

6. Shrewsbury. From this angle the flimsy construction of the rolling-stock of the period is even more apparent. Modern metal framed coaches can withstand very much greater impact without disintegrating. (*Illustrated London News*)

gradient as here – would have been deflected on to the sharp curve. The Mail was the exceptional case in which engines were not changed at Grantham, but the normal procedure was followed. After the accident the working at Grantham was changed and the points were kept set for the main line until each train had come to a standstill.

But why did the driver fail to make the scheduled stop? Rumours abounded of course: he was drunk; he had gone mad; he was taken ill. The latter was the most popular solution since he had had to leave a turn of duty the previous June with an attack of sciatica. Signalman Day's evidence, however, would seem to dispose of that theory.

More likely, it seems that his mind had wan-

dered. Every car driver knows how hard it is to maintain a hundred per cent concentration all the time. We understand these things better today. And the fireman? He was a much younger man and would be reluctant to question his superior's judgement – at least until the last moment when it would have probably been too late. There is a case on record of a driver who toppled to his death where a bridge had been removed, because his fireman was too terrified to tell him he was on the wrong line.

At Moorgate the Underground train ran into a blind wall at the end of the line killing the motorman and forty-two others. At Bourne End in 1945, as related in Chapter 11, forty-three was again the death-toll when a train was derailed while taking a crossover at speed. In all three accidents there were reports of the drivers standing apparently transfixed just beforehand. That, together with the fact that no definite reason was ever established for any of the trains behaving as they did, has inevitably lent an air of supernatural mystery to all three events for those so inclined.

Salisbury, Grantham, and now, just over a year later, Shrewsbury. For yet a third time a night express became derailed on a curve by a station, killing both enginemen and many others. At Shrewsbury the curve was at the approach to the station instead of beyond it, but otherwise the circumstances were almost identical. It happened on 15 October 1907 just after two in the morning. On this night the West of England Mail careered down the two miles long, 1 in 117 bank towards the station, passing signals at danger. It reached the curve at fully 60 mph – the restriction was ten. The locomotive was Experiment class no. 2052, 'Stephenson', and it struck the facing points at the approach to the platforms. Its wheels being suddenly deflected to the left, the effect was the same as at Salisbury. The engine keeled over on its right, skidded for a distance and came to rest on its side some twenty or thirty yards from the platform end. The first two vehicles were totally destroyed; the third was thrown aside and landed twenty yards away, while the next six coaches piled up in a heap behind the engine. Eighteen lives were lost: eleven passengers, two guards, three post office sorters, besides the driver and fireman.

This third accident in the 'runaway' series caused considerable public commotion, and on the first day of the inquiry Mr Lloyd George himself, still President of the Board of Trade, took his seat beside the Inspecting Officer, Col Yorke. He questioned the Crewe locomotive foreman closely about Driver Martin's hours of duty. His questions were not unreasonable for at that time, long before the introduction of the eight-hour day, railwaymen were often called upon to work excessive hours. Martin's hours

had not been excessive, but he had been out of bed for the whole of four out of the previous six nights, and several letters to the Inspector from retired enginemen put their finger on the spot. They gave personal experiences of going to sleep for a few minutes on the footplate; often, they pointed out, drivers did not manage to get proper sleep during daytime rests. There was no other possible explanation. The autopsy conclusively ruled out sudden illness and no trace of alcohol was found.

Without too great a flight of fancy we can picture those last moments on 'Stephenson's' footplate. Martin has dozed off, his hand still on the regulator handle, which keeps him upright. Fletcher has not noticed that his driver is asleep, for he is busy filling the boiler and putting his fire in order ready for coming off at Shrewsbury. Suddenly Martin wakes up, or Fletcher wakes him; they see the Crewe Bank home signal at danger and realise that they are at the bottom of the incline and travelling much too fast to be able to pull up for the junction curve. At this moment they would probably be doing not less than 75 mph, for the Experiment class, despite their smallish 6' 3" coupled wheels, were free-running engines downhill. Desperately Martin applies the brake and puts his engine into reverse, while he also manages to sound a series of warning blasts on the whistle. But all is of little avail to reduce speed much in the distance. There comes the moment of horror when 'Stephenson' turns over, then oblivion. Very probably a similar scene had been enacted at Grantham.

Shrewsbury was the last of the 'Midnight Runaways', as they became known, but alas by no means the last time a train would take a curve too fast and come to grief with such tragic consequences.

2
The High Pennines

HAWES JUNCTION (Midland Railway)
AIS GILL (Midland Railway)

The Settle and Carlisle line of the old Midland Company is probably the finest piece of railway engineering in Britain. There is a gradient profile of the highest stretch accompanying Chapter 17 on page 90. This gives some idea of the enormous undertaking it was. The line offers unequalled railway panoramas for those who are prepared to climb. I have stood on the summit of Whernside and watched three goods trains chasing each other up the Long Drag to Blea Moor; I have sat with my feet dangling over the scarp of Wild Boar Fell, whence I could almost have dropped a stone on the toy trains at Ais Gill, nearly 1,200 feet below. I have followed the course of the 'Thames-Clyde Express' for many miles as it made its way up the Eden valley, only to be brought to a stand at Mallerstang box by a laggard goods which ought to have been shunted at Kirkby Stephen.

This grim but glorious country was the scene, within three years and about two miles of each other, of the two worst disasters in the history of the Midland Railway. The first occurred in the early hours of Christmas Eve, 1910, about one and a half miles north of Hawes Junction, the station later known as Garsdale – now derelict and called at only by an occasional special train. Though the immediate cause was a signalman's forgetfulness, it was indirectly due to the Midland Company's small engine policy.

On the Settle and Carlisle line this meant that all expresses above a moderate weight had to be piloted up to the summit at Ais Gill, 1,169 feet above sea level; southbound from Carlisle, forty-eight miles away, and northbound from either Hellifield or Leeds, the latter sixty-four miles distant. The pilot engines were turned at Hawes Junction, three miles south of Ais Gill, to return light to their home shed. When traffic was heavy, as at holiday times, it meant that Hawes Junction was a busy place.

So it was on this Christmas Eve. It was a pitch black night and raining as it so often does in the High Pennines – a drenching downpour of fine rain. Whipped by a north-west gale this was driving against the windows of the signal box, where Signalman Sutton was having to cope with no less than nine light engines, which had arrived from Ais Gill during the previous hour in strings of four, three and two. The last couple were class 2 rebuilds, nos. 448 and 548, based in Carlisle; the remainder, bound for Hellifield or Leeds, were a fine typical bunch of ancient Midland locomotive power, including four rebuilt 4–4–0s of 1877 vintage, a whole clutch of which had come to roost at Hellifield.

7. Hawes Junction. All that would burn did in the fire that destroyed most of the midnight express. One of the gas cylinders that fed the flames can be seen in the top left hand corner. (*Illustrated London News*)

The time was 5.20 am; Sutton had been on duty since eight o'clock the previous evening and was due to be relieved at six. The two Carlisle engines had been turned on the famous stockaded turntable – the only one in Britain which needed a fence to protect it from the wind. At this moment they were waiting on the back platform, the one used by the North Eastern trains from Northallerton, for a down excursion to pass. Meanwhile two of the Leeds engines were turned ready to move off, and a Hellifield engine, 4–4–0 no. 312, ran up to the turntable.

The excursion ran through. As soon as it was clear Sutton moved the Carlisle engines across to the advance starting signal on the down main line. He could have dispatched them as soon as the excursion had passed to Ais Gill, and no doubt he intended to do so. But he was pre-occupied meanwhile with the up line, on which two fast goods trains were due, and with getting away the light engines for Leeds. The two goods trains ran through at 5.20 and 5.43, after which Sutton dispatched the two Leeds engines.

By this time the two Carlisle engines had gone out of Sutton's mind. He should have been re-minded of them by one or other of the firemen under Rule 55, which instructs a driver waiting an unusually long time at a signal to send his fireman or guard to the signal box. The rule was devised for exceptional situations, and at Hawes Junction it was normal practice for returning light engines to run up to the down advance starter behind an express that had just passed. They never had to wait more than four to six minutes, the time that it took for an express to clear Ais Gill. It was thought unnecessary to carry out an emergency procedure for a regular operation, especially as the engines were in full view of the signal box. So at Hawes Junction light engines did not observe the rule. Drivers Scott and Bath in charge of nos. 448 and 548 were expecting to be sent off at any moment.

Meanwhile at 5.39 the midnight express from St Pancras had been offered from Dent. It had carried a fairly full load as far as Leeds, but there were only fifty-six people left to go forward, including seventeen in the sleeping cars. Because its weight of 207 tons was 27 tons over the un-piloted limit for class 2, no. 549 was given a pilot, no. 48, an old Kirtley 2–4–0 which had spent its life on the Settle and Carlisle line. The express had made a special stop at Skipton and was running sixteen minutes late. It was now travelling at about 60 mph on the lofty stretch of level that precedes the final short climb to the summit. Sutton obtained acceptance from Ais Gill and pulled off his signals. The time was 5.44.

When the advance starter came off the two drivers of the Carlisle engines, who had been waiting for about twenty minutes, naturally took it for their signal. They 'popped' their whistles and moved off. Whether Sutton could have heard them in that wind, or seen them properly through his rain-bleared windows, is open to question; at all events he did neither. So he was surprised when Driver Tempest of no. 312 came into the box with a very odd look on his face.

From the turntable Tempest had seen it all. He had seen the light engines run across, then wait, then move off under the express's signals. A minute or two later the express passed through, and was lost to sight in the cutting beyond. Tempest turned to his mate. 'How far have them engines got?' he asked. 'It would have taken them all their time to clear Moorcock Tunnel,' his fireman answered. He had hardly spoken when the long scream of a whistle was borne down upon the gale from the north. 'He's catched 'em,' said Tempest, and went up into the box. 'What have you done with those two engines?' Tempest asked. 'They've gone to Carlisle,' Sutton replied. 'They've not,' Tempest retorted. 'When you pulled off for the down express them two engines was standing on the down road behind the advance starter waiting for it to come off, and when it came off they went.' Sutton laughed incredulously, but a look at his train register, and a call to Signalman Bellas at Ais Gill, told him what he dreaded to know. He looked out of his box to the North, where the low-hanging clouds had turned to an angry red. 'I've done it,' he said. It was now nearly 6 am and Signalman Simpson, who was due to relieve Sutton, had come into the box. 'Will you go to Stationmaster Bence,' said Sutton, 'and say that I am afraid I have wrecked the Scotch express.'

Drivers Scott and Bath had got a mile or more on their way and were travelling easily at about 25 mph. They were in the neighbourhood of Lunds viaduct when Bath, looking back, saw something which he could hardly believe – the lights of the express in the Moorcock Tunnel behind them. A moment later the express burst out of the tunnel, the engines throwing sparks high in the air as they pounded up the 1 in 165 gradient at 65 mph. When he had recovered from his surprise, which it would seem he was slow in doing, Bath opened his regulator and his whistle, while Scott hearing him did the same.

8. Ais Gill. Class 4 no. 996 heading an up Scottish express past the scene of the crash in which sister locomotive no. 993 failed to make the grade with such tragic consequences. (*Illustrated London News*)

Driver Oldcorn of no. 48 did not see Bath's tail light at once; drifting steam and the mist-like rain, together with the obstruction of the Grisedale Crossing footbridge, obscured it from his view. So the two engines were hardly more than a hundred yards apart – say six seconds' travelling at a net speed of 40 mph – before the drivers realised the danger. It was only then that either of them took action, far too late to have much effect.

The two light engines were driven forward for several hundred yards, Bath's engine minus its bogie, before they overturned at the mouth of Shotlock Hill Tunnel. Nearly two hundred yards behind them both engines of the express went over against the side of the cutting, and the first six of its coaches followed them. The two front coaches were telescoped and completely wrecked; all the dead were in these two. Apart from the two sleeping cars, the whole train was fitted with Pintsch oil lighting, the gas being stored in cylinders beneath the coaches at a pressure which at this moment was about 80 lb per square inch. The high pressure main pipe on the leading coach was broken, and the escaping gas was ignited by the showers of sparks from the derailed bogies and displaced brake gear. A shepherd in a cottage nearby saw a blinding flash as the gas took fire. Fanned by the strong head wind, the fire quickly enveloped the entire train.

Though dazed and badly hurt in the leg, Bath quickly picked himself up and walked through the downpour to Ais Gill box to warn the signalman. Meanwhile Johnson 2–4–0 no. 250, which was running light, tender first, from Carlisle – what a journey in such weather and on a practically unprotected footplate! – had passed Ais Gill at 5.55, seven minutes after the accident. Driver Judd noticed nothing as he approached the scene, for the fire had not yet appeared on the surface of the wreckage, but Oldcorn managed to attract his attention by sounding the whistle of the derailed no. 48. Judd halted alongside – the leftward derailment had left the up line clear – and emptied the water from his tender onto the now flaming debris, but the fire had taken too firm a hold. When Stationmaster Bence came up from Hawes Junction on a goods engine to draw the two rear vans to safety, the remaining vehicles, which were buffer-locked and immoveable, were burnt out.

Twelve passengers perished in this disaster. Three were never identified and are buried in Hawes churchyard. The Inspecting Officer, Major Pringle, placed prime responsibility for the accident on Signalman Sutton, which the latter had admitted from the first. The two light engine drivers, Scott and Bath, were also held to be gravely at fault in not carrying out Rule 55. 'I hold it is no good excuse for men to say that they were momentarily expecting the signal to fall,' wrote the Inspector. Bath's conduct after the accident, however, was highly commended.

On the subject of gas lighting the inspector was surprisingly equivocal. Gas has many advantages over electricity as a source of illumination, wrote Major Pringle, and he recommended making it safer by means of stronger cylinders and cut-off valves which would act in the event of the main pipe breaking. 'But,' he concluded, 'I still hold that electricity is the more desirable and should be adopted wherever possible.' Elsewhere in his report he referred to a device known as the track circuit. It was invented in America in 1872, but made no great headway in this country until the turn of the century. The principle of the track circuit is this: a section of rail is insulated at rail joints from adjoining sections. A low voltage current is passed continuously through the rails; this operates a switch or relay which is normally maintained in the closed position. When a train enters the insulated section it short circuits this current and opens the switch, and the train's presence is revealed by an indicator in the signal box. It will be seen that should the current fail, or an accidental short circuit take place, the device will behave as if there were a train in the section. Any failure, that is to say, would be on the safe side, an essential feature of any protective device. Had track circuits been installed at Hawes Junction the indicator would have shown 'occupied', and the presence of the light engines would have been revealed.

The Midland Railway took the Inspector's advice about track circuiting to heart, and after the Ais Gill accident three years later was able to claim that in this respect it had fulfilled his recommendations, but it needed that even more terrible accident to convince the Midland that gas lighting, whatever its merits, simply was not worth the risk. For here, once again, the night sky over the High Pennines was lit by the glare of a burning train. The fire was less destructive than at Hawes Junction, but the loss of life was greater.

The story begins at Carlisle, where two 4–4–0s, class 4 no. 993 and class 2 no. 446, were being coaled at Durran Hill shed. The coal was from a new source of supply; it was small, well impregnated with slack and was said to clinker easily. There had been constant grumbles by engine crews, though apparently no official complaints.

Thus Driver Nicholson of no. 993 was not reassured when he found that his train, a night express from Glasgow and Stranraer, was loaded to 243 tons – 13 tons above his engine's rated maximum – and he promptly asked for a pilot loco. There was one available but it was thought more time would be lost fetching and

attaching it than Nicholson would lose to reach the summit unaided. So he had to tackle the 1,100 feet climb to Ais Gill alone.

For a start he did well enough, but on the long stretches of 1 in 100 beyond Ormside, speed fell rapidly. By the time they had passed Maller-stang, the last box before the top of the climb, even though Nicholson was giving his fireman a hand with the shovel, pressure fell steadily. To prevent the brakes leaking on, he had to keep the large ejector working thus losing more steam. Finally, just half a mile from the summit and safety, the pressure was down to 85 lb and the train came to a standstill. Restoring pressure with a bad fire is no speedy task, and Nicholson admitted afterwards that he expected to be at least ten minutes. But when the front Guard Donelly came to enquire about the stop he told him: 'We'll be a few minutes.' By the time this had been relayed to the rear Guard Whitley, it had become 'Only a minute'. Whitley's duty

was to protect the train with detonators but, having received such a message, he did not bother to do so.

Back at Carlisle a little while earlier, Samuel Caudle, the driver of no. 446, had also made a protest about the coal. The load on his express from Edinburgh was only 157 tons however, 23 tons below the permitted limit, so he had no claim to a pilot. Caudle was fifty-nine; he had twenty-one years driving experience and a splendid record. In fact the typically solid, capable kind of engine driver that was nearly every boy's hero in the age of steam. His fire-man, Follows, was new to him and also, more pertinently still, new to the engine. This un-doubtedly had a bearing on what was to come.

Nearly a quarter of an hour after the other train set out, Caudle and Follows on no. 446 left to follow it. By the time they were approaching Mallerstang the engine was labouring. Where she should have been doing 30 mph or more she

23

was only making 20 to 25. At this point Caudle decided to go round the engine with his oil can. It was a routine with drivers to touch up the axle-boxes at least once between Carlisle and Leeds and this steep pitch was a favourite spot, because the engine was moving more slowly, while the short Birkett Tunnel offered brief protection from the wind. (As so often in the High Pennines it was a gusty night, but rainless.) Modern wick-type lubricators had rendered the trip quite unnecessary, but the established ritual had to be observed. Here Caudle showed the limitations of the traditionalist. With a strange fireman, bad coal and an engine losing speed, he should surely have known better than to leave the footplate. No doubt he expected to get back quickly, but the force of the wind delayed him, and by the time he returned they had run past the Mallerstang distant, and neither he nor Follows had seen it. It was of course standing at danger, since the Glasgow train had not been cleared back.

Caudle returned to find his fireman in trouble with the injector – a likely enough happening on a strange engine with this temperamental mechanism. Caudle set himself to put the matter to rights, and not too soon, for the water was near the bottom of the glass. He was busy with this just when he was passing the other Mallerstang signals. He did just glimpse the home signal at green, but that was the only one he saw and it turned out to be a false indication of safety.

Signalman Sutherland in Mallerstang box had been mystified; having had no clearance for the Glasgow train from Ais Gill, he had phoned his mate Clemnet there to ask where it was. But Clemnet, with the train out of his view, could only reply that he had no idea. Sutherland therefore had kept his signals at danger when he was offered the Edinburgh train from Kirkby Stephen. He had observed it travelling rather more slowly than usual, which had caused him

to think that it was obeying the distant and slowing down. He therefore lowered his home signal with the object of drawing it up to the starter. For this action he was severely criticised by the Inspector, but it should be said in fairness that he was misled by the low speed of the train, and surely a signalman is entitled to assume that a driver will observe all his signals.

So it was that the home signal showed a green light when Caudle approached it. As the express neared his box Sutherland realised to his horror that it was still steaming hard. He hurriedly returned his home signal to danger and waved a hand lamp frantically out of the window. But Caudle, pre-occupied with his injector, continued pounding his way up the hill. Not seriously worried about the missed signals, and blissfully unaware of the obstruction ahead, he was keeping a watchful eye on his new fireman's performance with the shovel. He would have done better to keep it on the road. Then his fireman called out: 'Look out, Sam, there's a red light ahead.' It was the tail lamp of the Glasgow train which Caudle, however, mistook for the Ais Gill distant, so he whistled for it to come off. He was barely 200 yards from the other train before he realised it was there.

Driver Nicholson of no. 993 had been standing for seven minutes. Looking back he saw a glow in the blackness; it was the red-hot smokebox of no. 446 as she was being thrashed up to the summit. Nicholson at once sent his fireman running back and Guard Whitley also belatedly started. Nicholson himself whistled and opened his regulator, but his train would not move. No. 446, steaming almost up to the last moment, smashed clean through the rear van of the Glasgow train and buried itself in the third-class coach next ahead. The roof of the van shot over the engine and broke open the front compartments of the Edinburgh train, in which a number of passengers were injured, though all the deaths were in the Glasgow train. The engine was smothered in wreckage, so completely that one of the rescuers did not realise it was there until the fire had burned the woodwork away. For just as at Hawes Junction, fire broke out almost at once. There was some doubt about its origin, but Col Pringle, as he had now become, concluded that it was caused by the escape of gas from cylinders under two of the wrecked vehicles. Since Hawes Junction the Midland had followed the Inspector's easier alternative and had begun to fit its stock with protective valves, but the coaches involved were not so fitted. Extinguishers were brought into use, but the flames took a firm hold and the three rear vehicles of the Glasgow express were burnt out. No. 446, the debris burnt off her, stood on the rails not greatly damaged, but with her red paint scorched white by the heat.

Sixteen passengers were killed in the crash, or died later from their injuries. At the enquiry the Midland's General Manager, Sir Guy Granet, was at pains to justify the Company's decision to continue building gas-lit carriages. He gave as the reasons: (1) the small number of fires after collisions proved to be caused by gas, (2) the adoption since these cases of various protective appliances, and (3) 'gas is a better light, and has considerable railway advantages' – meaning that it was more convenient and cheaper. Sir Guy, however, was fighting a rearguard action and the Midland yielded to the pressure built up by the two Pennine accidents. After Ais Gill no more gas-lit carriages were built.

The jury's verdict at the main inquest held Driver Caudle, Fireman Follows, Guard Whitley and the Locomotive Superintendent at Carlisle all guilty of negligence, the last named for failing to provide a pilot. The Coroner refused to accept this and the jury retired four times in all before they reached an acceptable verdict: death caused accidentally and by mis-

adventure. They had made it plain that they were not prepared to put anyone in the dock, meaning in particular Driver Caudle. It looked as if he was in the clear.

Alas for Caudle. One passenger, Sir Arthur Percy Douglas, had died in hospital at Carlisle, and the Deputy Coroner there left his jury in no doubt as to what sort of verdict he expected. The jury complied, and Caudle was arrested and was released on £50 bail.

Caudle stood his trial at the Cumberland Assizes before Mr Justice Avory, a judge notorious for his harshness. His summing-up was unsympathetic and the jury returned a verdict of guilty, with a strong recommendation to mercy. Before passing sentence the judge delivered himself of the following *obiter dicta*: 'I have to bear in mind that I sit here not so much for the purpose of punishing a particular offender as for the purpose of deterring others from offending in a like manner' – as if any driver needed to be deterred from putting his own life in danger.

The sentence, however, was lenient enough: two months imprisonment. The verdict and sentence caused intense indignation among railwaymen and there was talk of a strike. But the Midland management, its conscience pricked perhaps by the thought of its own part in the affair, did the handsome thing. It agreed to pay Caudle's wages while he was in gaol and to reinstate him thereafter. In fact he was released almost at once.

Just as Hawes Junction had highlighted a gap in safeguards against a signalman's failures, so this accident did likewise with regard to those of drivers. Nearly fifty years later, as we shall see in the last chapter, it was to be the failure of maintenance staff that would add a new category of accident to the story of the line over the High Pennines, where the drama of the scenery is matched by its history.

3
Quintinshill
(Caledonian Railway)

A quiet lowland rural location in Dumfries-shire, in the undramatic sunshine of a fine spring morning, was the unlikely setting for the greatest slaughter in the history of Britain's railways.

Saturday, 22 May 1915, dawned fine and clear on the Border, giving the promise of a glorious day. The war had been in progress for nine months, but it had brought no change to the life of Signalman James Tinsley, except to make him busier in his box at Quintinshill, about a mile and a half to the north of Gretna station. This morning he was on the 6 am shift, which meant getting up earlier than suited either him or his mate George Meakin, who shared the duties turn and turn about. So the two had worked out a scheme to give each other an extra half hour in bed. After six o'clock the night shift man would write the train register entries on slips of paper, which the day man could copy into the book when he arrived about 6.30. The arrangement was of course quite unauthorised, but it had worked successfully for a couple of years. For Tinsley, who lived in the railway cottages by Gretna station, it was especially handy on those days when the 6.10 am slow from Carlisle was shunted onto the loop at Quintinshill (where there was no station) to let a couple of night expresses from Euston pass. These were due out

of Carlisle at 5.30 am and 6.5 am, and if they were late the local was sent on ahead, as it had a connection to make at Beattock. When this happened the signalman at Quintinshill would send a message that 'the boy would get a ride today', which the Gretna man passed on to Tinsley.

So it was this morning. Tinsley duly mounted the footplate of the local at Gretna, creeping round the back of the train in case the station-master should be astir early. At Quintinshill traffic was building up. The down loop was already occupied by the 4.50 am goods from Carlisle, which was likewise waiting for the expresses to pass, while waiting to enter the up loop was a returning 'Jellicoe Special', one of the trains which carried coal from the Welsh pits to the Grand Fleet at Scapa Flow, and for which there was no room in the sidings at Carlisle. So there was nothing for it but to put the local train across on to the up line; this had happened on the average about once a month.

Tinsley jumped off the engine – no. 907, of the Cardean class – as it was being shunted through the crossover. He found quite a party in the box, for in addition to Meakin there were three train-men from the waiting goods trains. Tinsley immediately applied himself to the register, in which there were fifteen entries to be made – five

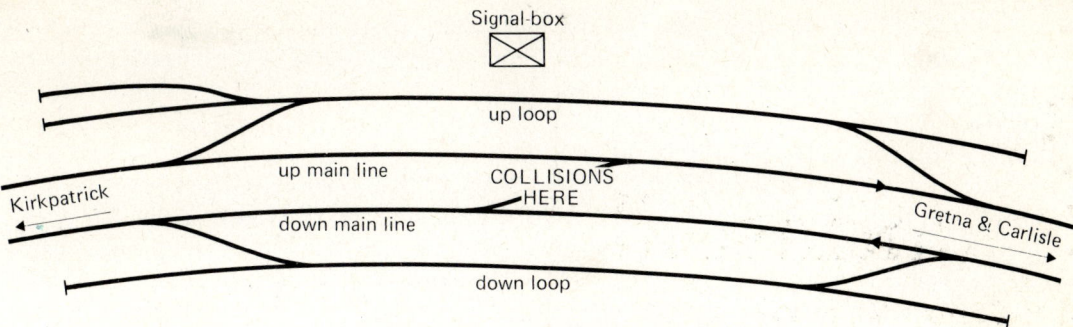

Figure 2. Quintinshill: track layout

The diagram shows (top to bottom): Signal-box, up loop, up main line, COLLISIONS HERE, down main line, down loop. Kirkpatrick is to the left, Gretna & Carlisle to the right.

each in respect of the three trains which had passed since six o'clock.

Meakin meanwhile accepted the empty coal train on to the up loop, and clearance was given to Kirkpatrick box to the north, though whether by him or Tinsley was never established. The first express, which had left Carlisle at 6.27, was then accepted from Gretna and ran past.

What Meakin failed to do was to protect the local. A train standing on its wrong line can obviously become a source of danger, and a series of safeguards have been devised to prevent the possibility of a collision. In the Caledonian's case the first safety device consisted of a lever collar – a bright red object slipped over the lever to remind the signalman not to pull it – but Meakin did not place one on the up home signal lever. This was not just a lapse of the moment; he told the inquiry that the collar was hardly ever used in the box. Before condemning him let us recall that the Companies themselves were not agreed on whether the collar was necessary or even desirable. More serious was Meakin's omission to take the second protective step, namely to send the 'Blocking Back Within Home Signal' code and set his train indicator at 'Train On Line', which would have prevented Kirkpatrick from even offering another train. There was company in the box, and the war news to discuss from the morning paper which

Tinsley had brought; these distractions no doubt caused him to forget.

Enter another neglectful party. Fireman Hutchinson of the local came into the box to remind the signalman and sign the train book, as required by Rule 55. But under the Rule he should have made sure, before leaving the box, that his train was properly protected, and this he omitted to do. 'My train was right outside the box,' he said later. 'Tinsley could see it there.' Which was true enough, if Tinsley had been looking, but that individual was still busy with his writing. He also probably had his back to the window; such at least is suggested by the layout of the box, which was unusual in having its frame at the rear.

At 3.42 that morning the first of two troop trains had left Larbert for Liverpool. They were conveying the 1/7 Royal Scots, a Territorial battalion drawn from Leith and Musselburgh, to embark on the troopship 'Empress of Britain' en route for the Dardanelles. The battalion had been earmarked for France, but the ill-fated Gallipoli campaign was going badly, and so it was being diverted there. This first train consisted of A and D Companies, together with the CO and the headquarters staff – 498 officers and men. Troop trains are not noted for their luxury appointments; this one consisted of fifteen vehicles borrowed from the Great Central Railway, mostly old six-wheelers with wooden frames, in which the men were travelling, with all their kit, eight to a compartment. Six Caledonian vans were attached at the rear for the baggage. The driver, Scott, a Carlisle man, was something of an aristocrat among drivers, for he had driven three generations of Royalty – Victoria, Edward VII and George V. He was in charge of McIntosh superheated 4–4–0 no. 121 as he and his fireman set out upon their last journey.

It was 6.43 at Quintinshill. Meakin, off duty now, was sitting reading out the war news to the company in the box. From Kirkpatrick came the bell signal offering the troop train. Tinsley, preoccupied with his writing, had forgotten all about the standing local and he had nothing to remind him. He accepted the troop train. At 6.47 he obtained acceptance from Gretna and pulled off his signals. About the same time he accepted the second express from Carlisle, and cleared his signals for that also.

Now here is a remarkable fact. On the spot were six enginemen trained in the art of reading signals, as well as three guards and two signalmen; eleven railwaymen in all. Yet not one of them noticed that the signals had been cleared for the troop train while the local was standing in its path.

On the troop train Driver Scott was travelling fast down the 1 in 200 gradient. The obstructing local first came into view when he was 280 yards away – nothing like distance enough in which to bring his train to a stop. What attempt he made to do so will never be known, but the train was still moving at a high speed when it struck the local. Contemporary accounts, based on survivors' stories, suggest that the effects of this first collision were relatively slight, but this can hardly have been the case. No. 907 was driven back forty yards and came to rest with her tender across the down line. The engine of the troop train was flung on its side across both running lines. The foremost of the Great Central carriages shot clean over its engine and landed some distance in front of it, and the remaining carriages were spread-eagled over both tracks. A 213-yard train was compressed into 67 yards. It was a major catastrophe in its own right.

Meakin was just leaving the box when the collision occurred. 'Whatever have you done, Jimmy?' he cried out. 'What can be wrong?' exclaimed Tinsley. 'The signals are all right.' Meakin reminded him of the local that had been waiting on the up line. Then, as a new and horrifying thought struck him, Meakin shouted: 'Where is the 6.5?' He rushed to put the down signals to danger. The same thought also struck Guard Graham of the local, who had quickly picked himself up from the floor of his van, as well as to the driver and fireman of the coal empties train. All three started to race up the line waving their arms, Graham in the lead. Too late. Graham had covered 167 yards in thirty-one seconds – not bad for a middle-aged man – when the express was upon them. At its head were 4–4–0s nos. 48 and 140, the latter as pilot to Beattock summit, and the engines had worked up to a good sixty on the gently falling track out of Carlisle. Both drivers saw the gesticulating figures; they shut off steam and applied the brakes. They could do little more, though, than check speed before ploughing into the wreckage, and into the soldiers who were escaping after the first collision. Just fifty-three seconds had elapsed between the two collisions.

The leading engines struck the tender of the troop train engine and drove it thirty yards through the wagons of the goods train on the down loop. Its own tender mounted the framing of the train engine, and the first three coaches were telescoped. On top of the heaped up engines was piled a vast mountain of debris, which caught fire almost at once. All the Great

Central coaches were gas-lit, and their cylinders had been re-charged just before leaving Larbert. Coals from the troop train engine ignited the escaping gas and soon the whole train was ablaze. Extinguishers, the water in the goods engines' tenders, water pumped from a local stream and the Carlisle fire brigade – all were powerless to check it. All that day and throughout the next night the pyramid of wreckage blazed, consuming the dead and the living alike.

Eye-witnesses were to describe the scene: the flames, not lurid as at night but angry and red; the billowing smoke grey-yellow in the bright sunshine, the hissing of the engines and the pop-popping of the ammunition from the officers' pistols.

The lucky ones were killed outright. Scores of others had to wait helplessly for the fire to reach them. Men burning to death begged their rescuers to shoot them.

The entire troop train was destroyed, save only the vans at the rear. These had broken away on the recoil of the first collision, and despite the gradient had run some distance up the line, where the brakeman of the empty coal train managed to secure them. The first three coaches of the express were burnt out, as well as seven wagons of the down goods and five of the empty coal train. Thus Quintinshill achieved another record: that of involving five trains. The fire

10. Quintinshill. In this newspaper picture the intensity of the fire gives some idea of the horror of the holocaust. (*Illustrated London News*)

11. Quintinshill. With the fires out at last, the complex and depressing business of clearing up goes ahead. An army officer wanders about – no doubt still stunned by the unexpected carnage at a time when death on a large scale was commonplace in his profession. A horse drawn cart takes away some of the debris – it needed man-made horsepower to create a scene like this. And above it all stands Quintinshill box – every signal in its domain now resolutely set at danger. (*Radio Times Hulton Picture Library*)

burned for over twenty-four hours and all the coal in the engines' tenders was consumed. The last bodies were brought out on the Sunday afternoon, but more portions of bodies were recovered later.

In this disaster 226 people perished – more than in any other two British railway accidents put together. Of these 214 were in the troop train, seven in the express, two in the local (which was nearly empty), while three were railwaymen. The third, besides Driver Scott and his fireman, was a sleeping-car attendant in the express. Both crews of the express escaped miraculously with bruises; the driver and fireman of the local took refuge under the empty

coal train as the troop train bore down upon them.

Few of the survivors among the troops escaped injury. When the remnant was paraded at 4 pm only fifty-four were there to give their names. The two companies in the second train were sent on to the Dardanelles, where they quickly suffered heavy casualties.

Of the engines concerned, no. 121 of the troop train was damaged beyond repair. No. 907, one of only seven heavy 4–6–0s owned by the Caledonian, was scrapped after an attempt had been made to repair her.

Most of the injured were taken to hospital in Carlisle. Some died on the way, others after arrival. Since they had died in England an inquest had to be held, and the jury returned a verdict of manslaughter against Tinsley, Meakin and Fireman Hutchinson. This raised a curious legal point. The Coroner said he had no choice but to commit the men to the Cumberland Assizes, although their lawyer argued that he had no power to do so, since the alleged offence had been committed in Scotland. But the men

30

had already been charged by the Dumfriesshire police, and thus made legal history by being indicted for the same offence in both the English and the Scottish courts.

All three stood their trial in Edinburgh in the following September on the charge that: by breaches of duty they caused the collision and thus did kill Frank Scott (the driver) and about half-a-dozen other named persons. The case against Hutchinson did not stand up and he was discharged. The two signalmen presented pitiful figures in the dock. They had suffered, said their counsel, in shocking fashion. Both had had nervous breakdowns, and they had suffered from sleeplessness and mental anguish. Surely forgetfulness, pleaded Counsel, is not a criminal offence, however tragic its consequences, but the negligence had been too glaring and the results too terrible. Scottish juries do not have to be unanimous but this one was, and it was out for only eight minutes before returning a verdict of guilty. Tinsley, who was held to bear the greater blame, was sentenced to three years imprisonment, and Meakin to eighteen months. In due course mercy prevailed, and both men were released after they had served a year. They had already been sentenced to the greater punishment of a life-time's remorse.

Quintinshill box is no longer there. It was demolished along with those at Gretna and Kirkpatrick after the line was electrified – part of the Euston to Glasgow Inter-City route. There is power signalling now, controlled from the electronically equipped boxes at Carlisle and Motherwell. The loops are still there, however, and are in fact included in the electrification, but they are all that remains to identify the location. The scene of Britain's worst-ever rail disaster has all but been erased.

4
Abermule

(Cambrian Railway)

The Cambrian Railway was one of the minor pre-grouping companies which traversed those parts of Wales where none of the greater ones had found it worth while to extend. Its main line ran from Whitchurch in Shropshire to Aberystwyth, and it wandered over the country's desolate interior from Brecon in the south to Pwllheli in the north. Where industry and population abounded, there the Cambrian was not. Save for an outlying branch to Wrexham, it served not a single town with as many as 20,000 inhabitants. It was in short a poor and not very efficient railway, until the Great Western took it over at the grouping and gave it a face-lift.

The now-closed station at Abermule, lying between Montgomery and Newtown in what is now known as Powys, was just a little bit more than a wayside station because it was the junction for a short branch line to the market town of Kerry. Like the whole of the Cambrian, the line was single, with passing places at most of the stations. It was worked under the system invented by Edward Tyer, who must certainly have imagined that he had evolved a foolproof method of preventing collisions on a single line. Its essence is that its operation requires action by the signalmen at both ends of a single-line section. The tablets giving the train authority to proceed are locked in an instrument, and a tablet can only be withdrawn if the man in charge of the instrument at the other end presses a plunger. When a tablet has been taken out an electrical circuit is broken, and a second tablet cannot be withdrawn from either instrument until the first tablet has been replaced in the instrument at the other end, or has been returned to its original instrument.

You would have thought that such a system could not possibly go wrong, but Tyer had reckoned without the gang of incompetents at Abermule.

This quartet consisted of a signalman, Jones, and two youngsters, the porter Rogers aged seventeen and an odd-job lad of fifteen called Thompson, together with the man in charge, relief Stationmaster Lewis, doing duty for the regular man Parry who was on holiday. Of the four we have the clearest picture of Thompson, a simple lad, willing but dim; in the words of the Coroner, the sort of lad who was ready to oblige the stationmaster or signalman if they felt disinclined to move about. Now it will be obvious that the Tyer system demands that only authorised persons shall work the tablet instruments. The authorised persons in this case were the stationmaster and the signalman, but a go-as-you-please system had grown up whereby

12. Abermule. The wreck of the express with its 'Pwllheli and Shrewsbury' roof-board still in place on one of the coaches. Rescue workers cluster round one of the carriages in which most of the casualties occurred. (*National Railway Museum*)

anyone did the job who happened to be at hand. For this the regular stationmaster Parry was responsible, but his stand-in Lewis had accepted these casual methods without question: doubtless they were not confined to Abermule. Here, however, there was a special circumstance. The tablet instruments, instead of being in the signal box, were in a room by the booking hall on the opposite platform. It saved Jones' legs therefore to send one of the boys to withdraw or replace a tablet, in which case they would also sign the train book, likewise strictly against the rules.

Thus it had gone on for a long time. In the twenty years and more since the Tyer system had been installed on the line there had never been an accident, and nobody contemplated the possibility of one. In a way, its apparent infallibility proved to be its greatest weakness. That certainly seems to have been the case at Abermule on 16 January 1921.

Two trains were due to cross at the station about mid-day: a down (westbound) slow and an up train booked to run non-stop from Newtown to Welshpool. Though Abermule was the normal crossing point, this might take place at either Montgomery or Newtown if one or the other train happened to be late. On this day the relief stationmaster Lewis was away at dinner, while Rogers and Thompson were having theirs in the booking office. Jones was in the instrument room nearby. At 11.52 am the slow was belled from Montgomery; Jones accepted it and plunged on the instrument to enable his colleague there to release the tablet. Jones entered

'Train Entering Section' at 11.55 am. He then phoned Moat Lane Junction, the station on the far side of Newtown, to inquire as to the whereabouts of the express. He was told that it had just gone by. He then left for the signal box, having told Rogers that the slow had left Montgomery three or four minutes before and that the express had passed Moat Lane, thus making it clear that he was expecting them to pass at Abermule. He then opened the level crossing gates and pulled off the down home signal.

At this point Lewis returned from his lunch, but neither Jones nor Roberts told him that the express was between Moat Lane and Newtown. His habit was to be on the platform when the trains crossed, but on this occasion he found waiting for him Permanent Way Inspector Thomas, who wanted a wagon for loading some stake wood. Thomas was in a hurry, for he wanted to be away by the slow train, so Lewis went down with him to the goods yard.

Meanwhile at 11.56 the express had been belled from Newtown. With no one else about Rogers went to the instrument room, acknowledged the bell signal and plunged on the Newtown–Abermule instrument to release the tablet at Newtown for the express. He had done this many times before and it did not occur to him to tell anyone. He then went off to the ground frame at the west end of the platform to set the road for the express.

At 11.59 'Train Entering Section' was belled from Newtown. Lewis was in the goods yard, Jones was in the signal box, Rogers was at the ground frame; where Thompson was is not related. At all events there was no one to acknowledge Newton's signal, which was not entered in the train book.

At 12.02, when the slow train arrived, Thompson was there, and since no one else was about he collected the tablet from the engine crew. At this point Lewis came hurrying up from the goods yard, having heard the train arrive. Thompson handed him the tablet with the words: 'Change this tablet, Frank, I am going to collect the tickets.' That at least is what he intended to convey, but he had an impediment in his speech and Lewis thought he had said, 'Take this tablet, the train is going on.' So Lewis assumed that Thompson had already changed the tablet under orders from Jones. Lewis asked where the express was and the half-wit Thompson replied: 'About Moat Lane', presumably because he had heard Jones say so some minutes earlier. With that the lad went off to collect the ticket from the solitary passenger who had alighted. Lewis assumed the express was late and told Thompson, who had now returned, to go and tell Jones to pull off for the slow train. It was all very haphazard, but since the train crew had not yet been given the tablet it was not necessarily fatal. The next piece of carelessness was. All tablets are marked with the sections to which they refer, and it did not occur to Lewis to look and see if he was handing over the right tablet. Nor did the fireman think to examine it; he took it without removing it from its pouch. With that Lewis gave the right away.

Meanwhile Rogers could not understand why he could not move the ground frame levers. They were locked from the signal box, and naturally could not be moved for the up loop line while the down starting signal was off. Rogers does not appear to have noticed this signal and after some hesitation he was about to shout to Jones to release the signal box lever when he saw Lewis give the down train the right away. If the stationmaster gave it, he thought, it must be in order, and he assumed that the express must have been held up at Newtown.

What a catalogue of wrong assumptions! With a light-hearted disregard of all the rules, two trains had been set on a collision course from which nothing could save them.

After the train had left, Thompson went into the instrument room to bell 'Train Entering Section' to Newtown. He looked at the instruments. The Montgomery–Abermule instrument had not been cleared, while the Abermule–Newtown one showed that a tablet had been withdrawn for the express. He called Lewis, who rang Newtown in haste. 'Has the express left yet?' he asked. 'It left at 11.59,' came the reply. In a despairing attempt Lewis 'waved' the up distant signal, i.e. put it quickly up and down, in the hope of attracting the slow driver's attention, but probably the train was already past the signal.

The collision took place about a mile from Abermule. At what point the crew of the slow train saw the express, if at all, will never be known, for both were killed. They could not have been keeping a good lookout, for their engine was steaming up to the moment it struck the express.

Driver Jones and Fireman Owen of the express, on the other hand, were fully alert. Running downhill at about 50 mph Jones first saw the slow train some 300 yards away, belching exhaust as it laboured up the bank at 30 mph or so. He did what he could in the few seconds available. He shut off steam and applied the brake, slowing his train appreciably as the other came heedlessly on. When it was about two engines' lengths away he and his fireman jumped.

The effect of the head-on crash was horrifying. The locomotives – both standard Cambrian

13. Abermule. The remains of the local train's 4–4–0 twisted almost beyond recognition, rises above the merged rolling stock of the two trains. (*National Railway Museum*)

4-4-0s – were fantastically twisted. The boiler of the express engine was wrenched from its frame and thrown beside the track facing in the opposite direction. The engine of the slow train reared straight on end like a bucking horse. In the space of fifty yards both engines and five coaches – four from the express and one from the slow – normally occupying 110 yards, formed a tangled mass of wreckage. The express suffered the worst, and most of the fifteen passengers killed were in its second and third coaches.

Jones somersaulted three times as he jumped and landed up underneath a carriage. His neck was badly cut but he was not otherwise seriously injured and his first thought was to retrieve the tablets. He called out to his fireman, who although also hurt began to search among the wreckage and eventually found both – his own and the Montgomery–Abermule one, telling its own fatal tale. 'Oh Tom,' he told his brother as, he lay in the infirmary that night, 'I am so glad there is no blame attached to me. It was I who took the tablet at Newtown.'

In his report the Inspecting Officer, Col Pringle, had some scorching criticisms to make of methods at Abermule. It was impossible to hold the two youths responsible. The inquest jury pinned the blame on Lewis and Signalman Jones, though it may be thought that the regular stationmaster Parry, who had allowed the lax working to grow up, was lucky to escape. The jury's first verdict was to find Lewis and Jones guilty of gross neglect, but the Coroner reminded them that this was equivalent to a verdict of manslaughter, which had not been their intention. So they retired again and came back with the verdict that the two men were guilty of great neglect calling for very severe censure, which the Coroner proceeded to administer.

Both Lewis and Jones were seen to be in tears as the Coroner addressed them.

5
Hull Paragon
(London and North Eastern Railway)

We speak of the million-to-one chance, but if there is such a thing as an infinity-to-one chance, this was it. A signalman had three-tenths of a second in which to make a once-in-a-lifetime mistake, and in that split fraction of time he managed to make it. It happened at the approach to Hull Paragon station on the morning of 14 February 1927, when an outgoing train to Scarborough was diverted onto the wrong line and collided with an incoming train from Withernsea. On the diagram the numbers shown are those of the levers in the Park Street box. No. 171 is the C road signal, i.e. for outgoing trains; the other three numbers are points. I have shown only the numbers with which we are concerned.

We must now move to West Parade Junction, 480 yards further out. The 8.22 am from Withernsea, in the charge of NER class F 4–4–0 no. 96 and filled with office workers and school-children, was approaching the junction at about 15 mph. It was running about nine minutes late. Driver Dixon had already shut off steam for the stop and had his hand ready on the brake handle. Spanning the junction is the Argyle Street road bridge, and as he emerged from underneath it Dixon raised his eyes to look for the West Park starting signal, which was at clear. On dropping his eyes again he was confronted by the spectacle of a train approaching him on the same line a mere couple of engine lengths away. He only had time to apply the brake before the trains collided.

Driver Atkinson was in charge of M class no. 1628, very similar to class F, on the 9.05 am Hull to Scarborough. He came out of the station

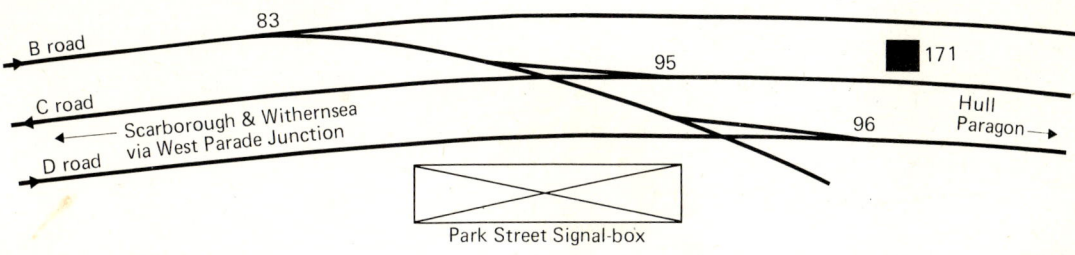

Figure 3. Hull Paragon: track layout

37

14. Hull Paragon. Scarborough-bound M class no. 1628 with its tender encased in the forward vehicle of its train – giving some impression of the force of the impact of a head-on collision even when the combined speed is no more than 15 mph. (*Illustrated London News*)

along C road and at the Park Street home gantry received the centre of the three signals, no. 171, applicable to a straight movement along the road. He noticed nothing unusual as he went by Park Street box, though he might have done. It was only when he lost sight of the West Park home signal, which ought to have been clearly in view, that it seemed to him there was something wrong. A water crane, too, on the right seemed closer than it should have been. Atkinson crossed over to the fireman's side and then back to his own. There could be no doubt about it. Somehow or other he had been put across onto the incoming B road, the road along which the Withernsea train was approaching. At this moment no train was in sight, but Atkinson lost

no time in shutting off steam and applying the brake. The next thing he knew was a violent impact, which buried him in a shower of coal from the tender. He had very nearly brought his train to a standstill.

Compared with Abermule it was a very mild collision. There the combined speed of the trains was probably near 60 mph; here it was about 15 mph. Neither engine suffered much more than front end damage, but both trains were extensively telescoped and twelve passengers were killed. The majority of the dead were in the Withernsea train and although most of the coaches in both trains were gas-lit, there was no fire.

Let us see what had been happening in the Park Street box. This was worked by the electro-pneumatic system, which had been installed twenty-one years earlier and which, among other advantages, considerably eases the

15. Hull Paragon. F class no. 96 on the right, locked with its fellow 4–4–0 as if in deadly combat. (*Illustrated London News*)

signalman's labours. It was manned by three signalmen, who took turns three weeks at a time to act as chargeman. In charge on this day was Alfred Campling, who was actually the junior of the three, with his two assistants, Clark and Gibson. Clark was the eldest; he had forty-six years' service and in him we discern the authentic conservative with a small 'c'. He did not hold with this new-fangled electro-pneumatic apparatus, and half-believed, I think, that it went wrong at times through sheer cussedness. This did not affect his actions, but it certainly affected his attitude afterwards. 'I know that the points do not do as they ought to do,' he told the inquiry.

The Withernsea train was due to be put across from B to D road via points 83 and 96, thus crossing the path of the Scarborough train on C road. 'Right away Scarborough,' called out Campling to his assistants, 'and B to D for Withernsea as soon as the Scarborough is out.' Gibson returned signal 171 behind the Scarborough train, while Clark set the road for the Withernsea train. The operation was performed at speed, for since the Withernsea train was already late the signalmen were anxious not to delay it further. According to the rules, Gibson should have waited to restore 171 lever until the whole train had passed the signal, though in my observation this is a rule which is seldom strictly observed by signalmen. In this case Gibson restored the lever when the engine and the first three coaches, out of five, were past. Whatever the letter of the rule, he was acting with the good of the service in mind. If only he had been able to foresee the result of his couple of seconds' premature action!

As the Scarborough train passed, the signalmen heard a curious clicking noise in the frame, and then, as it was running out of sight, Gibson said, 'Where has that chap gone?' 'What chap?' asked Clark, to which Gibson replied: 'Well, I thought that Scarborough looked a bit too far over.'

A few minutes later Driver Atkinson came into the box. When he had extricated himself from the coal he had sat down on the ballast for a few minutes to recover, then he set off for the box. 'What are you playing at this morning?' he asked Campling. The latter turned to Clark.

'Did you pull that lever over?' he asked. Clark made no reply. Atkinson saw that the signalmen, as he put it, were a bit flustered, so he said no more and left the box.

How had the Scarborough train got transferred to B road? It could only have been through the no. 95 points. Yet these points were interlocked with signal 171 so that when the signal was at clear the points were locked in the straight position. Moreover they were equipped with facing point locking bars – long bars placed ahead of the points which are depressed by the wheels of a train. This locks the points and prevents any movement just before and during the time when the train is passing over them. Yet in spite of this double precaution no. 95 points had been pulled over. After much careful investigation the Inspecting Officer, Col Pringle, found the answer. When no. 171 signal was restored, before the train had fully passed, this had freed the interlocking. At that moment, the Inspector calculated, the train was 37·81 feet from the facing point locking bars, when the points would again have become locked. Tests indicated that the train had been travelling at 13·75 mph, so that it would have covered the distance in 1·9 seconds. For that period of time no. 95 points were free. During that time Clark must have moved them in mistake for no. 96, an action which, including the moving of the locking bar lever, was timed to take 1·6 seconds. Three-tenths of a second sooner or later, and disaster would have been averted. Three-tenths of a second for Clark's mistake, possibly the only one of his career, to prove fatal. A one-in-infinity chance if ever there was one. If Gibson, too, had waited for the passage of just one further coach before restoring the lever, the engine would have been on the locking bar and safe.

Now the clicking noise which the signalmen had heard was explained. It was made by lever 83 and its connections as the Scarborough train ran through the trailing points which were set against it.

The Inspector ascribed the accident to the human factor, though Clark stoutly denied that he had pulled the wrong lever, and instanced various cases in which the electro-pneumatic system had gone wrong. I doubt if he was ever really convinced that it was not the system, but himself, that was to blame.

6
Sevenoaks

(Southern Railway)

Of all the bad summers of the century the villainous season of 1927 ranks high. It never seemed to stop raining. Such weather means an anxious time for the permanent way staff, for it seeks out any weaknesses in the track and demands constant vigilance by the maintenance gangs. So in this derailment at Sevenoaks we may name the weather as the chief culprit. But not, I think, the only one; the track itself was faulty. Was the locomotive design faulty too? It is that question which gives the accident its particular interest.

Among the pre-grouping companies the South Eastern & Chatham was not one of the shining lights, but it did have some good locomotives. These included some German built 4-4-0s. When the Great War precluded getting more from that source, the big step was taken of deciding to build a 2-6-4 express tank engine of their own. The prototype, no. 790, appeared in 1917, but for some reason no more were built until 1925 after the company had become part of the Southern, when they were named after south country streams and became known as the River class. Some had two outside cylinders and some three cylinders; for tank engines they had the large-sized coupled wheels of 6′ diameter, which meant a high centre of gravity. Compared with a tender engine, a tank engine is inherently less stable, at all events at speed. The mere absence of a tender deprives it of one stabilising influence, while the water in the tanks is liable to surge, despite the baffles. Moreover there is the problem of springing. Two thousand gallons of water weigh about nine tons, which means that the weight on each coupled axle could vary by as much as three tons. The River class was rather lightly sprung, an excellent feature for a good track, because it means the engine is less hard on the road. But the South Eastern & Chatham track was far from being in the top class. When the Rivers were multiplied the first batch was loaned to the Brighton section, where they performed with complete success, but back on their own section they were soon in trouble. Drivers complained of their rolling at speeds at above 50 mph. It was noticed that the rolling tended to be worse in wet weather, and on certain stretches of the line. It is hard to understand why this proclivity was not discovered while no. 790 was at work alone, but it was not, for whatever reason.

Nor was it merely a matter of rolling. There had been actual derailments, though without serious consequences. In the previous March no. 890, 'River Frome', had come off the rails at Wrotham, while on 2 August no. 800 had done likewise on a sharp curve at Maidstone. Only four days before the Sevenoaks accident no. 890 came off the road again with its whole train near Bearsted, although since it was travelling slowly the train did not overturn and no one was hurt. This accident was ascribed to track subsidence caused by rain. Most ominous of all, one of the class even became derailed at speed, but miraculously re-railed itself. Only the tell-tale marks on the sleepers showed what had happened. In view of these mishaps it can hardly be said that the Sevenoaks accident came as a surprise.

24 August was a typical 1927 summer's day. There were three storms over London; in Kent it rained all the morning, though it had stopped by two o'clock. On this day the 5 pm from Cannon Street to Minster via Deal, first stop Ashford, was in the charge of Driver Buss on no. 800, 'River Cray', which had come off the line at Maidstone three weeks before. It was hauling an eight-coach load, including a Pullman, well filled with returning City workers. Buss knew all about the River class and its rolling. Having breasted Knockholt summit at about 35 mph he was anxious, he said, to keep the speed of the train within limits on the four-mile descent to Dunton Green, which begins with over two

16. Sevenoaks. River class no. 800, 'River Cray', nestles against the embankment on which it came to rest. They are digging out the front wheels which had become wedged in under the track. (*Radio Times Hulton Picture Library*)

17. Sevenoaks. Pullman car 'Carmen' rammed broadside across the Shireham Lane overbridge. Seeing the state of it here makes it seem all the more remarkable that none of its occupants was hurt. As in other accidents, the superior construction of Pullman vehicles was, no doubt, largely responsible for that. Imagine what would have happened to most of the other coaches seen in pictures on previous pages. (*Radio Times Hulton Picture Library*)

miles through the Polhill tunnel at 1 in 143. At the same time he warned his fireman, who was new to the class, to put on some coal while in the tunnel, so as to avoid being thrown about the footplate as the train gathered speed. Rather surprisingly, Buss kept his regulator partly open right down to the foot of the bank, by which

time the train was certainly travelling at more than 60 mph, though Buss estimated only 57.

Dunton Green was a well-known rolling spot for these engines. This time the roll was thought to have been set up by trailing points beyond the station, and it became intensified as the train traversed the embankment which crosses the floor of the Darent valley. Then the engine crew heard an unusual knocking sound in front. The nearside leading coupled wheel had mounted the rail, on which the flange marks showed for twenty-three feet before they dropped over the side. The knocking was the sound of the wheel striking the chairs and on hearing it Buss immediately closed his regulator. When the knocking still continued he applied the brake also.

At this point the gradient changes to 1 in 160 up, and the line enters a deep chalk cutting on a left-hand curve. Had this cutting been un-obstructed Buss might well have been able to pull up his train on the rising gradient. Un-fortunately a road bridge, spanning the cutting at a skew angle with a pier between the lines, proved a fatal obstacle. By the time it reached the bridge the engine was swaying violently; a passer-by on the bridge said it seemed to be roll-ing about a foot to either side.

The partially derailed no. 800 struck the bridge on both sides as it swayed. The left-hand cylinder and front corner of the engine struck the abutment, while the right-hand side of the cab scraped over the centre pier. The engine ran on for over 100 yards further, taking the leading three coaches with it, and all came to rest leaning against the steep side of the cutting. The fourth coach was crushed and jammed under the arch, while the Pullman behind it was thrown broad-side against the central pier. Strange to relate, no one in the Pullman was hurt. Thirteen pas-sengers lost their lives in the accident. The driver, Buss, escaped with cuts, but his fireman was unconscious for two days.

It was the first pair of coupled wheels which became derailed, not the Bissel truck carrying the pair of leading wheels. Impossible as it might seem for an intermediate pair of wheels to leave the rails like this, the marks on the track proved that this is what had happened.

Which was at fault, the engine or the track? At the inquiry it was admitted that owing to the number of bad spots caused by the weather, maintenance had got into arrears. Without wait-ing for the official report of the accident the Southern Railway withdrew the entire River class from service, and in due course the loco-motives re-appeared as tender engines and gave no more trouble.

Who or what then was really to blame? No individual, surely, but rather a common weak-ness of railway organisation in the past; a lack of liaison between the locomotive and the engineer's departments. There are several instances where a new type of locomotive has fallen under the engineering department's ban and has had to be modified, or restricted in its range of routes, simply because the locomotive department did not take the precaution of finding out beforehand. In this case since the de-signer, R. E. L. Maunsell, was also the com-pany's Chief Mechanical Engineer, he should have known that his otherwise excellent engine was unsuitable for the less than perfect track it had to run on. As it was, the fact had to be estab-lished by a series of mishaps culminating in disaster.

7
Charfield

(London Midland & Scottish Railway)

Charfield station, now closed, lies on the former Midland Company's Derby to Bristol main line between the also closed stations of Berkeley Road Junction and Wickwar. Over the stretch between Standish Junction, near Stonehouse, and Yate the Great Western exercised running powers, which was not at all to the liking of the Midland.

Just before 5 am on Saturday, 13 October 1928, the situation was as follows. Shunted onto the branch line at Berkeley Road was a Great Western semi-fitted goods consisting of forty-nine loaded vehicles and a brake van hauled by 2–6–0 no. 6381. Ahead of it, in the lie-by at Charfield, was an LMS unfitted goods. This had picked up six loaded coal trucks at Berkeley Road and was now overloaded for the class 3 0–6–0 hauling it. Both these trains had been shunted to allow a passage for a parcels train from Leicester, which had now gone through. Coming up behind was the night Mail from Leeds to Bristol, with through postal vans from Newcastle, which had left Gloucester at 4.54.

Which goods should now have priority, the overburdened LMS train in front, or the faster-running Great Western one behind? On other lines the question would have been settled by the signalmen on the spot, but the Midland had a system of centralised train control, which had

been taken over by the LMS and under which the area controller took such decisions. It had been introduced to speed up goods traffic, and though it certainly had done that, it was said to be sometimes rather rigid in its operation. I was able to talk to some of the local participants at Charfield, and their accounts throw fresh light on the story. In particular Signalman Smith, who was on duty in the Berkeley Road box, told me of a circumstance that did not come out at the inquiry. He, and Harry Button at the Charfield box, advised that the Great Western train should go forward and the other one stay shunted at Charfield until both the Great Western and the Mail had passed. The Great Western could then have reached its own line at Yate Junction and got clear out of the way, whereas to send the LMS forward was bound to cause delays. However, the controller at Fishponds decided otherwise. He was a man, says Smith, who had been dismissed from Control during the war for the serious blunder of holding up an ambulance train, but had managed to get himself reinstated. One sees in him the typical rigid-minded functionary of the sort which had caused criticism of the system. So the LMS goods was sent on and there was no choice, short of delaying the Mail, but to put the Great Western train, when it reached Charfield, into the lie-by which

18. Charfield. The GWR 2–6–0 no. 6381 is still wedged under the bridge whilst its removal is discussed by the recovery team. In the foreground is the underneath of Driver Aldington's Johnson class 3 4–4–0 no. 714 where it came to rest in the middle of the up empty goods train after being deflected off the tender of no. 6381. (*Central Press*)

the other had just vacated. The LMS driver, however, decided without warning to take water, so delaying the Great Western train still further, before dragging his way up the hill to Wickwar.

The system of signalling at Charfield was the one standard on the Midland main lines, known as the 'rotary interlocking' block. The effect of this is that no train can be signalled into the block

in advance until the train ahead has operated a re-lease treadle at the next box, and the signalman there has accepted the second train on his block instrument. At Charfield, additionally, when the points were set for the lie-by normal inter-locking prevented the inner and outer home signals, and therefore the distant, from being pulled off. At the outer home signal was a track circuit.

The Great Western train duly arrived at Char-field, and Button called out to the driver that it was to be shunted into the lie-by. He set the points, and slowly Driver Gilbert began to back his fifty vehicle train off the main line. It had operated the release treadle before coming to a halt, thus enabling Smith at Berkeley Road to offer the Mail, which was now approaching that station. Button cleared back the goods at 5.13 and immediately accepted the Mail, which he was entitled to do under the regulations. His distant and both his home signals were locked at danger by reason of the points being set for the lie-by; this meant that the Mail would first be checked at the distant and then come to a stand at the outer home signal – on the track circuit – until the goods was clear of the main line.

The Mail, in charge of Driver Aldington, was hauled by Johnson class 3 4–4–0 no. 714, rebuilt with superheater: a class which had a life-span of over half a century and for many years bore the brunt of the express work between Derby and Bristol. Its train of eleven vehicles contained only four passenger coaches, marshalled at nos. 3 to 6, and carrying a night Mail's usual light load of about sixty passengers. Such secondary expresses are not held to warrant the most modern stock, and the passenger coaches varied in age from nineteen to twenty-nine years. Three out of the four were gas-lit, as well as five of the vans; the Midland's policy of conversion to electric lighting had made rather half-hearted progress in the fifteen years since Ais Gill.

The down line had recently been relaid between Berkeley Road and Mangotsfield, and a 45 mph restriction was still in force. Aldington, however – though he denied it later – kept going at about 60 mph. It was good travelling, one must agree, against the rising trend of the road. Aldington was probably trying to recoup a four minutes' late start from Gloucester. There was nothing dangerous in such a speed, but it chanced that the minute or so gained precipitated the accident.

Here is Aldington's story of what happened next, as he told it at the inquiry. It was foggy in patches, he said. Approaching the Charfield distant he crossed over to the left side of the cab and was able to read it at eighty yards' distance, when it was showing a clear green. Fireman Want, too, though unused to the road, saw the signal at sixty yards and called out: 'He's got it off, mate.' Between the distant and the outer home the fog became thicker, but with the distant at clear (said Aldington) he carried on with the regulator open, though he admitted missing both home signals. He had never been checked at Charfield before and would be expecting a clear run. Is this yet another instance of a railwayman's imagination leading him astray? Signalman Smith, who saw a good deal of Aldington in the days that followed the crash, does not think so. His view is that Aldington had become drowsy, possibly as a result of a few drinks before starting out, and had dozed off – as we have supposed happened to Martin at Shrewsbury – so that he saw no signals at all. As for the fireman, as Smith puts it, he would hardly know whether he was at Berkeley Road, Charfield or Wickwar.

Button at Charfield was watching his track circuit indicator. He saw it change to 'occupied' as the Mail reached it and then to his consternation it changed back to 'clear'. With the goods still not clear of the main line, the Mail had run through his signals. In agony Button clutched his head in his hands, awaiting the calamity he could do nothing to prevent.

Driver Gilbert had practically finished propelling his train into the lie-by. Ten seconds later and the whole train would have been safely stowed away, but at Charfield every circumstance was unlucky. The two leading wagons were still on the points when no. 714 caught them and then struck the back of the Great Western engine's tender. If the collision had taken place on an open stretch the results would have been serious enough, but just where the lie-by diverged there is a substantial brick overbridge to constrict the space. By a further evil

19. Charfield. Removing the mangled chassis of one of the Mail's burnt out coaches from the other side of the bridge where they had piled up. The tender of the GWR locomotive is lying on the points over which it was reversing into the lie-by. The dent made by no. 714 as it struck and overturned the tender can be clearly seen. Note too, on the parapet of the bridge, the skeleton of the section of carriage roof that was hurled onto the road by the impact. (*Central Press*)

where it drove through seven or eight of the empty goods wagons before coming to rest leaning against the cutting side. Its tender, the Great Western engine, and the smashed trucks became wedged together in a compact mass under the bridge. Against this solid obstacle the Mail's five leading vehicles piled themselves in a tangle of wreckage. The fifth vehicle – one of the passenger coaches – was forced up against the side of the bridge and part of its roof shot into the roadway.

Sixteen passengers died in the disaster. Some of the dead, probably most, were killed instantly. A cloud of gas from the broken cylinders was ignited either by coals from the engine or sparks, was fed by more gas escaping from fractured connections, and within minutes the wreckage had become a furnace. The first six vehicles of the Mail, including all four passenger coaches, were burnt out. The two front wagons of the goods train with all their contents and a number of empty wagons were also destroyed.

Both Aldington and Want had miraculous escapes, but the guard of the Mail, Millier, was less lucky. He was travelling in the rear van, the only vehicle to remain undamaged, but he was thrown forward by the shock and dislocated his shoulder. The Post Office sorters came off badly too. Their vans were behind the passenger coaches and kept the rails, but thirteen of them were injured, as were both the Great Western enginemen.

Half an hour after the accident Aldington went up into the signal box. The distant, he told Button, was off. 'Impossible,' replied Button. Aldington pointed to the repeater: sure enough it was showing 'off', but that furnished no backing for his story. It was found that wreckage had fallen on the wire and driven it right into the ground, thus pulling the repeater into the 'off' position. The Inspecting Officer, Col Sir John Pringle, investigated every possibility that

chance an LMS up empty goods train was passing at that moment. No. 714 bounced off the Great Western tender, which overturned to the left, and shot across the tracks to the right, might have caused the distant to be showing clear, including the chance that some article from the goods train might have fallen onto the wire – but he could find nothing. Short of the fantastic assumption of some nocturnal practical joker, the case was proved.

So Col Pringle brushed aside Aldington's story and held him responsible for the crash, and in a lesser degree Fireman Want, whom he described as an unreliable witness. Aldington appeared before the magistrates at Wotton-under-Edge who had to decide at what point negligence becomes criminal. The magistrates took only five minutes to decide that there was no case to answer, and Aldington was formally acquitted at the Gloucester Assizes. He was luckier, we may think, than Caudle at Ais Gill, who was far less blameworthy.

So Aldington departed to Bournville, to spend the remainder of his driving days on shunting engines.

Back for a moment to Signalman Button, who had had to wait helplessly for the crash. The sequel is something I should not dare to set down had I not had it from Signalman Smith at first hand. I give it as nearly as may be in Smith's own words: 'I saw Button on the Sunday, the day after the accident. There was nothing unusual about him then. When I next saw him a few days later his black hair was streaked with white. "Have you put your head in a white paint pot, Harry?" I asked. "No, my boy", he replied, "that's where I put my hands on the top of my head when I saw the crash was coming. It's the result of the shock coming out."'

8
Castlecary

(London and North Eastern Railway)

The scene is the wayside station of Castle-cary, on the Edinburgh and Glasgow line of the former North British Railway, in the murk of a snowbound winter twilight. The date is Friday, 10 December 1937 and the time 4.37 pm.

The accident record of the North British had been an unhappy one. In the previous thirty or so years there had been six serious accidents killing in total more than forty passengers. Castlecary overtopped them all. With its thirty-five dead it ranks third in the list of the worst Scottish railway disasters; Quintinshill and Tay Bridge of course being first and second.

It had been snowing all day at Castlecary, on and off. As darkness fell it was still snowing fairly thickly, reducing visibility to something under 500 yards. An east wind had driven the snow against the faces of the down line (Glasgow-bound) signals, rendering their lights almost invisible.

At Gartshore, three block sections ahead in the Glasgow direction, a pair of facing points had been put out of action by the snow. This had happened about four o'clock and the down line was closed for half an hour. By that time two trains were held up in rear, a passenger train at Croy and a goods at Dullatur East, the next station to Castlecary. Two Glasgow-bound expresses were due to follow, the 2 pm from Dundee and the 4.03 pm from Edinburgh. Signalman Smith at Dullatur had intended to

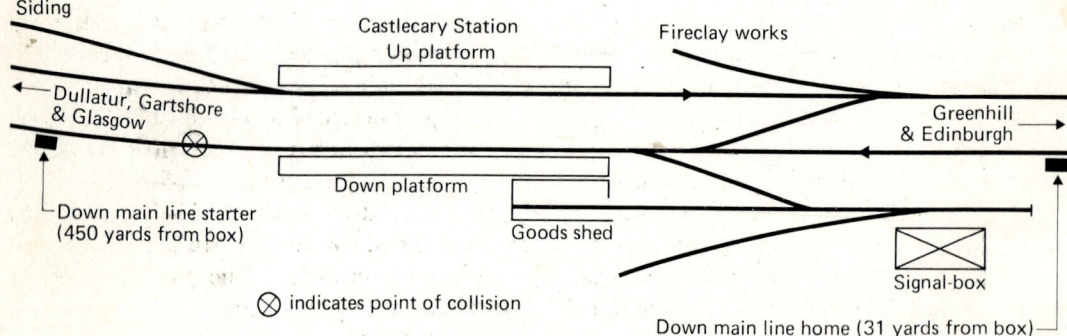

Figure 4. Castlecary: track layout

20. Castlecary. No. 2744, 'Grand Parade', the A3 Pacific of the Edinburgh to Glasgow express, embedded in the embankment under the ruins of the third carriage of its train. (*Illustrated London News*)

clear a path for them by shunting the goods onto the up line, but this could not be done until two up passenger trains had passed.

The scene moves to the footplate of no. 9896, 'Dandie Dinmont', a D29 4–4–0 at the head of the Dundee express, on a train of seven bogies with a fish van at the rear – the latter with a consignment that was to have gone by road, but was switched to the railway at the last moment. Driver Macaulay was peering out through the snow for a sight of the Castlecary distant signal. Even at 150 yards he could still not see the signal light, but against the darkening sky he caught sight of the snow-whitened semaphore arm, standing – he was quite positive – at clear. He was travelling at about 55 mph and despite the weather was only two minutes behind time. He missed the home signal (which was at danger) because his attention was attracted by a red lamp being waved from the signal box. He braked on the instant, and brought his train to a standstill with the tail 269 yards from the box. There was a track circuit behind the starter, on which the greater part of his train was standing. The time was 4.30. When he had pulled up Macaulay sent his fireman Fleming to the box to find out the cause of the stop.

Up in the box the signalman, Andrew, as I will call him, had noticed that the Dundee train was not reducing speed as it approached the home signal at danger. Hurriedly he had waved a red light from the window and blown his whistle, but the train had gone by, as he imagined, still steaming. He had followed its course until the tail-lamp was half-way along the platform at which point a corner of the goods shed cut it off from his view. In his alarm he had not noticed that it was slowing down. If he had glanced at the track circuit indicator immediately in front of him he would have seen it was showing 'occupied', but instead he had sent the 4–4–5 'Vehicles Running Away On Right Line' signal to Dullatur, and followed it up with a phone call.

Having done this, Andrew bethought himself of the Edinburgh train, which had been offered from Greenhill Junction. As he was momentarily expecting word of a collision at Dullatur, it seems extraordinary that his mind should be occupied with accepting a following train. However, Andrew was a theorist rather than a practical signalman and had studied the rules to the point of obsession. The 4.03 from Edinburgh was an important train, he reasoned, and he must not hold it up unless there was a regulation that justified his doing so. He could think of none and a call to Signalman Beattie at Greenhill Junction confirmed his opinion. So he cleared back the two o'clock ex Dundee and accepted the Edinburgh train at 4.32. The fact that a collision at Dullatur would have held up the train anyway does not seem to have crossed Andrew's mind.

During the three minutes after 4.32 Andrew dealt with one of the passenger trains on the up line, and according to his own account he twice tried to phone Control, but the line was engaged both times. He did nothing to try and find out whether or not the expected collision had occurred – that was the Dullatur man's business!

At 4.35 Fireman Fleming of the Dundee train reached the box. Andrew was enormously relieved. 'Thank God you've stopped,' he said, and went to the phone to tell Smith at Dullatur that the train had stopped in the section. Fleming corrected him. 'We are standing at the starting signal,' he said, but Andrew got the impression – or said he did – that Fleming had said: 'Through the signal'. Fleming signed the Train Register at 4.35, though the entry was afterwards clumsily altered to 4.38, by whose hand was never disclosed.

At 4.36 came the 'Train Entering Section' signal from Greenhill Junction, a short one and three-quarter mile section. 'I'll have to see about getting the four o'clock stopped,' he said. He took up a hand lamp and some detonators and hurried out of the box, followed by Scott and Fleming. They only had time to fix one detonator properly when A3 Pacific no. 2744, 'Grand Parade', at the head of the 4.03 came roaring out of the snowstorm, bearing down on them at a speed of nearly 70 mph.

In charge of 'Grand Parade' was Driver Anderson. Like Macaulay eight minutes earlier, Anderson was peering out to catch sight of the Castlecary distant. It had grown that much darker and he was travelling faster. He was something under 100 yards away when he managed to observe the arm, standing distinctly at clear. On that point he was as positive as Macaulay. As he passed the signal he looked back and caught a second glimpse of it by the light of the open fire door. He missed the home signal at danger, but saw the red hand lamp that Andrew held up to him from the lineside and moved to apply the brake. Then he heard the crack of the detonator and saw the tail light of the Dundee train ahead. He made a full brake application but could do little more than slightly check speed. 'Hold on,' he called out to his fireman, Kinnear, as he braced himself for the crash.

The fish van at the rear of the Dundee train disintegrated, its providential last-minute attachment probably saving a few lives. The two coaches ahead of it were destroyed, and all seventeen passengers in them killed, as were five others in the next coach (the fifth) – a total of twenty-two out of the 110 passengers in the train. There was no telescoping; as Sir Nigel Gresley put it afterwards, the two rear coaches were simply squashed. The whole train was pushed forward fifty-two yards and Driver Macaulay was badly injured.

'Grand Parade' for its part ploughed up seventy yards of track and came to rest on its side embedded in the embankment ninety-six yards from the point of collision. The bodies of the three leading coaches parted from their bogies, which piled up behind the tender and formed a ramp by means of which the first two coaches shot clean over the engine and landed upright beyond it athwart the tracks. The third coach came to rest twelve feet in the air, on top of the engine and tender. Considering that there were 200 passengers in the Edinburgh train, the number of dead was remarkably small; six in the leading coach and seven in the second.

The coaches of both trains had buck-eye couplings, which help keep derailed vehicles in

21. Castlecary. Seen from the other side, only the tender of 'Grand Parade' can be clearly distinguished. Some idea is gained here of the terrible power of the momentum that sent the train's first two carriages shooting over the engine leaving the third perched on top. (*Fox*)

line. They also prevent over-riding and thus inhibit telescoping. All but the front three coaches of the Edinburgh train remained in alignment, as did the front four of the Dundee express. The last three coaches of the second train actually stayed on the rails, and passengers stepped out of them onto the platform at Castlecary unaware that there had been a collision. As one lady wrote: 'I did not suffer from shock at all, as it only seemed to me as if the train had been pulled up badly.'

Anderson and Kinnear had remarkable escapes. The former was not injured at all; the latter after being trapped in the cab and reported killed was rescued with a slight wrist injury and a burn on his cheek, caused by acid dripping from the battery of the coach above.

Meanwhile Andrew was telephoning to Beattie to check the times of the Train Register entries. He told Beattie that he had 'got everything', meaning that he was clear of blame as far as the rules were concerned.

Much later, at about six o'clock, the injured Macaulay managed to drag himself to the box. He wanted to know the position of that distant. 'Have you a repeater on that distant?' he asked.

53

'No,' replied Andrew. 'You gave me a clear signal,' said Macaulay. At this Andrew exploded in righteous indignation. 'Oh, don't come that stuff,' he said. 'All right, there's no use getting angry about it,' replied Macaulay, and limped out of the box.

No one ever discovered what the distant was showing, not even the Inspecting Officer, Lt–Col Mount, though he spent a great deal of time trying to find out. That the distant could have been showing a true clear was ruled out by the fact that the home and starting signals were at danger. Furthermore, it was proved that weight of snow could not possibly have caused the arm to droop to anything like thirty degrees. The only explanation to fit all the evidence was that the arm had failed to return to normal when Andrew restored the lever at 4.09, and that was shown to be in the highest degree unlikely. Had both drivers been in error, or was the signal, for whatever reason, showing clear? Without actually expressing an opinion, the Inspector intimated that he preferred the drivers' evidence to Andrew's.

There was much less doubt about the position of the track circuit indicator, which Andrew had failed to notice when he thought that the Dundee train was running away. He maintained that he had looked at it afterwards and that it was showing clear when he phoned Beattie; the latter confirmed that Andrew had told him so. When after the accident the indicator showed 'occupied' Andrew tried to suggest that the Dundee train must have moved back, and when that explanation failed he resorted to the assertion that it must have been showing a false clear. The circuit was tested afterwards and found to be in perfect working order.

The main feature of the case, as the Inspector pointed out, was Andrew's acceptance of the Edinburgh train two minutes after he had supposed the Dundee train was running away and was about to collide with the goods. It is difficult, wrote the Inspector, to believe that a responsible signalman could do such a thing, still less plead justification because block telegraph regulations do not prohibit such action.

Both drivers were criticised for driving at a speed possibly in excess of that which was justified in the adverse weather conditions, though the Inspector's strictures were mild enough. Who then, if anybody, might have expected to find himself arraigned after the accident? Not Andrew. However, it would seem that someone in authority demanded a scapegoat, and the choice of victim fell on Driver Anderson. If the Inspector's report had been available a charge could hardly have been brought, but where Court proceedings are involved the report is not published until after they are concluded. So it contains a footnote, which I quote verbatim: 'Before the Lord Justice-Clerk, in the High Court of Justiciary at Edinburgh, and a jury of nine women and six men, Driver D. J. Anderson was tried on a charge of culpable homicide on 30 March. The Lord Advocate withdrew the charge on 31 March, the jury was directed to return a verdict of "Not Guilty" and Driver Anderson was discharged.'

9
Norton Fitzwarren
(Great Western Railway)

Those who had to do much travelling in World War II remember the nightmare of journeys in the blackout. The crowded trains, the dim lighting, the incessant delays, made train travelling, which should be a pleasure, into a hell. We had little thought to spare for the even harder lot of the railwaymen, short-staffed and handling a swollen traffic, and not least that of the enginemen, blinkered in their anti-glare screens and with many of their familiar land-marks invisible. It is remarkable that throughout the war we have only two really major disasters to record. Both took place during the blackout.

Although we encountered one of its trains at Charfield, we come now, for the only time in this book, to the Great Western Railway itself. That that Company had such a clear record was in no sense due to chance. From 1906 it had developed its system of automatic train control (ATC), with audible warning to the driver, applied at the distant signal. This consisted of a ramp on the track not electrically energised when the signal was at caution, in which case a siren sounded in the cab and the brakes were partially applied. If the signal was at clear the ramp was energised and a bell sounded. It was this system which Inspecting Officers pleaded in vain, in one accident report after another, for other Companies to adopt.

So for half a century up to 1940 the Great Western had been practically free from serious accidents. The last grave one had also been at Norton Fitzwarren in November 1890, when a broad gauge Cape Mail special had collided with a stationary goods train which had been shunted and forgotten by the signalman; ten lives were lost.

It was fifty years almost to the day and, by one of those extraordinary coincidences, at the exact spot, that the long immunity ended. At 3.47 am on 4 November 1940 the 9.50 pm night express from Paddington to the West of England ran through junction trap points onto open ground with the loss of twenty-seven lives.

The 9.50 was headed by King class no. 6028, 'King George VI' (originally 'King Henry II'), with a thirteen-coach train, jam-packed as usual with 900 passengers aboard. In charge was Driver Stacey, of Old Oak Common shed. It had left Paddington while the 'blitz' was actually on, which meant that it would have had a slow passage in the early stages. Travelling by the long route via Bristol it dragged its weary way into Taunton at 3.30 am, an hour and eight minutes late. Meanwhile the 12.50 am news-paper train, taking the direct route via Castle Cary (not to be confused with the Castlecary of our last accident), with a featherweight load of five vans and likewise hauled by a King, was running ahead of schedule. It was not due to stop at Taunton. With four tracks through Taunton from Creech St Michael to Norton Fitzwarren, Wadham, the signalman at Taunton West Station box, decided to let it through on the fast line and dispatch the express on the relief one – something that had been seldom, if ever, done before. The principal down platform at Taunton, where the express stopped, being actually on the relief line, it was a matter of sending the train forward on the same line instead of crossing it over again to the main line in the normal way.

Here we encounter yet another case of a railwayman seeing what he expected to see. Driver Stacey had been accustomed to see the down-relief-to-main line signal come off at the platform end; this time, of course, it was the down relief line signal which was off. So he set off into the blackness all unaware that he was not on the main line as usual. As he passed the Taunton West Junction distant signal, on the same gantry as the Taunton Station West home, he thought he heard the ATC siren, though in fact he could not have done so. Great Western policy was to site signals on the left, although the driver sat on the right. But when the relief lines were added between Taunton and Norton Fitzwarren in 1931, insufficient space was available so the main line signals were placed to the right, between the down and up tracks. Had these signals, at which Stacey was looking, been in the normal position, he would have seen that they were on his right instead of his left. As it was, they merely appeared a little further to the right than usual, not far enough for him to notice the difference. They were, of course, the signals for the newspaper train, now close behind, which Stacey was reading as his own. His own signals on the left he did not observe at all, because it did not occur to him to look that way.

So 'King George VI' gathered speed until according to the speedometer – all the King class were so fitted – it was doing about forty as it approached Norton Fitzwarren. The convergence of the relief line with the main line is shortly beyond the station, and had the platforms been showing lights as in peace time it would have provided Stacey with a clue. In common with all other wayside stations, though, it was blacked out for the duration.

We now come to the inexplicable part. The two Norton Fitzwarren distants – there was an additional inner one – were of course at caution. The ATC apparatus at the outer distant – found afterwards to be in perfect order – must therefore have given its siren-cum-brake warning, which Stacey must have cancelled. However, he had no recollection of either the warning or the cancellation. Possibly this was the warning he thought he had heard on leaving Taunton, and he had got the time and place confused; at all events he did cancel it. Not for the first time, human fallibility had defeated the most elaborate safety devices. Only when the fellow King on the newspaper train drew abreast in Norton Fitzwarren station did Stacey realise his mistake. It was then too late to avoid an accident; the catch-points lay only 100 or so yards ahead. Catch-points at such a place prevent anything on a secondary line entering junction points when they are set against it, diverting it, in this case, off the rails and onto spare ground. 'We are on the down relief,' Stacey told his fireman, who

22. Norton Fitzwarren. The stricken King class no. 6028, renamed after the reigning monarch 'King George VI', with the wreckage of the worse damaged coaches behind it covering the crucial catch-points. The flooded conditions through which Driver Stacey waded waist deep are well in evidence here and must have hindered the rescue work too. Now, with the casualties taken away, it is a time for assessment and investigation. Norton Fitzwarren station in the background is again witness to a major accident just as it was almost exactly fifty years before. (*Central Press*)

was to die a few seconds later, and with that the engine went through the catch-points and onto the soft ground beyond, coming to rest nearly fifty yards further on. There I saw it thirty-six hours later, as I travelled down to the West. We passed the scene of the accident at reduced speed, so that I was able to have a good look. 'King George VI' lay canted over on its left side, with its front end buried in the ground.

The Great Western did not use buck-eye couplings and the first five coaches were scattered over all four tracks, but the remainder kept the rails and were undamaged. Of the twenty-six passengers killed, thirteen were naval ratings; considering the crowded state of the train it is remarkable that casualties were not higher. The left-hand overturn of the engine, which killed the fireman, enabled Stacey to climb out of the cab uninjured.

Like a good railwayman, Stacey's first thought was to protect the line. In this waterlogged countryside he waded waist deep back onto the tracks and made his way to Silk Mill Crossing box, a mile in the rear. There, agitated and dazed, he told the signalman that he was afraid he was responsible for the accident. At the inquiry the Inspecting Officer, Lt–Col Mount, dealt with him sympathetically.

Well might the death roll have been multiplied tenfold! For the end of the story is the tale of the most hairbreadth escape in the history of railway accidents. The enginemen of the newspaper train, behind their screens, were quite unaware that they were passing the express. So also was Guard Baggett, travelling in the fourth van. He was amazed when his window splintered and a metal object came hurtling through and struck him on the arm. Thinking there was something amiss with his train he applied the brake and brought it to a standstill at Victory Crossing, a mile further on. There he spoke with the driver, but as they could discover nothing wrong they decided to proceed cautiously to Wellington, where they learned of the accident.

The object which flew into the van was a rivet head from the bogie frame of 'King George VI'. Nor was that all. The panelling of the fifth van was scored with indentations made by the flying ballast as the express became derailed. The newspaper train had drawn clear in the nick of time. A second or two later and it would have ploughed into the packed carriages strewn across its path, to wreak a slaughter on the Quintinshill scale.

Even in disaster the Great Western's deserved good fortune had not entirely deserted it.

10
Eccles

(London Midland & Scottish Railway)

'Come,' said the porter at Eccles, 'and I will show you.' He led the way to the platform end and pointed to the retaining wall of the cutting just beyond. At a height of about a dozen feet the brickwork was broken and scarred. 'That's where the engine struck the cutting wall.' Thus has the Eccles disaster engraved its own memorial.

Eccles lies nearly four miles out of Manchester on the old Liverpool and Manchester line; an unlovely spot, seemingly made for fog and gloom, and it was in the fogbound blackness of the morning of 30 December 1941, that two trains collided outside the station. A down train from Manchester filled with workers, ran sidelong into an up train, likewise full, as the latter was crossing from the slow to the fast line. At the time of the accident the station clocks showed it had just gone 8.18 – exactly as those at Harrow and Wealdstone would eleven years later in the worst rush-hour crash of all. At Eccles, however, it was still dark at that hour for the war had meant that Summer Time was in force throughout the winter. There were yet thirty-seven minutes before the end of the blackout.

Here I must explain fog block working, which also figured at Harrow providing another coincidental link between the two disasters. Where there is a junction or conflicting train

movements, a train may in the normal way be allowed up to the junction home signal before being brought to a stop. It is thus allowed as far on its way as possible before being held up. But with traditional signalling an extra margin is called for in fog, and under fog block working the train would be held inside the signals of the previous box. (The procedure may vary somewhat from place to place, but that is the general principle.) Fog working at Eccles operated only in the absence of fogmen; once these were at their posts normal working could be resumed.

There were six fog posts at Eccles, but on this morning there were only three men available to man them. So these were allocated to the essential points which would enable fog block working to be suspended. The three fogmen rejoiced in the names of Parrington, Pantling and Patten. In the box at Eccles was a fairly new man, Signalman Lowe, and it is not surprising that he got the names mixed up.

The fog had been continuous for twenty-one hours, so that all three men had been out on duty the previous day for their full twelve-hour shift – the longest time allowed. The rule was that after this shift the fogman should have nine hours off – not an excessive rest period between two spells of such trying duty. In this case the fogmen had been withdrawn at ten o'clock the previous evening so as to be on duty again at 7 am, ready for the heavy morning traffic. Or rather, two of them had been withdrawn then; for some reason Patten, at the down distants – fast and slow – had not been recalled until 11.30 pm. So he was not due to resume until 8.30 am.

Fogmen going on duty had to report at the signal box either personally or by phone. Lowe expected Patten to phone and Pantling to report in person, or possibly he had already got the names confused. So when he heard a voice at 7 am saying: 'I am going on duty now, Charlie', he thought it was Pantling's. Whose voice it was remains a mystery, but it belonged to none of the fogmen. A minute or two afterwards Pantling phoned from the station, but Lowe thought it was Patten making his expected call – forgetting, if he was ever aware, that Patten was not due back until half past eight. The booking-boy, Acton, realised that it was Pantling, and so entered it in the register. He said afterwards that he had told Lowe that he had done so, but Lowe either did not hear or misheard him, nor did it occur to Lowe to look in the register. Parrington had meanwhile reported and had gone to his post at the down outer home signals. 'I have all the fogmen on,' remarked Lowe to Acton. 'We are all right now.' With that he suspended fog working.

The fog was specially thick at Eccles – owing, it was said, to the proximity of the Manchester Ship Canal – and visibility was down in places to no more than ten yards. Because of the fog both trains were running late: the down train twenty-seven minutes late and the up train forty-nine. Many of the workers should by rights already have been at their jobs.

The up train, hauled by LMS standard 2–6–4T no. 207 was being closely followed on the slow line by a train from Bolton, so it was decided to put it across at Eccles on to the fast line at the crossover at the Manchester end of the station.

Exactly at that moment a down train was approaching on the slow line at about 30 mph, having run past the distant and outer home signals at danger. Neither crew saw anything of the other train, though the fireman of the up train thought that he heard a swish as of a train passing. The next thing the crew of the up train knew was that they had been brought to a standstill by the breaking of the vacuum pipe. The down train, in the charge of 2–6–4T no. 2406, had struck the leading coach of the other train obliquely at the crossover. The locomotive tore through the carriages, completely destroying two and ripping off the sides of two others, finally coming to rest at an angle of forty-five degrees against the cutting wall and making the marks which the porter showed me. The leading coach of the down train was also destroyed. Altogether twenty-three people lost their lives.

How had the down train come to collide with the other? If fog working had been in force it would have been held at the previous box, Cross Lane Junction. But as we have seen, Lowe had suspended fog working in the belief that Patten was at his post at the down distants, and so had accepted the train to the outer home, which meant that the distant had remained at caution. The train had also run past the outer home, where Parrington was on duty. Why had it not been brought to a stop there? Here is the driver's story which he told at the inquiry.

After passing Cross Lane Junction (he said) he told his fireman to look out for the Eccles distant, which was on the latter's side. The fireman in evidence said the signal was showing green – possibly yet another instance of someone thinking he saw what he expected to see. Thus re-assured by his fireman, and further re-assured by the absence of a detonator, the driver accepted that the distant was at clear. He admitted, however, that though the fog post was on his side he had seen no one there.

At the outer home, the driver continued, he saw Parrington waving a green lamp. He described the lamp in detail: the flame was working up on one side as if the wick were unevenly trimmed. He had heard no detonator.

Parrington contradicted this story absolutely. He had held up a red lamp, he said, and the detonator was in position and had exploded. On the latter point he was supported by one Bowden, the tail lamp man at the Eccles box, who gave evidence that he had heard the detonator. The green light story was discounted by the fact that Parrington was standing on the far side of the fast lines, twenty-four yards from the train, and it was very doubtful whether in the dense fog the driver could have seen any lamp.

We have to conclude that the driver was lying, and embroidering his tale to make it sound convincing. The Inspecting Officer, Col Wilson, evidently thought so, for he said bluntly that he believed Parrington. As to the detonator at the outer home signal, he gave the driver the benefit of the doubt. The engine was running chimney first, and it was possible that the sound had been muffled in the tank engine cab. The driver, though, should not have delegated the duty of observing the distant signal to his fireman, and he was not proceeding with the care necessary in a bad fog. However, the Inspector put the main responsibility on Signalman Lowe. He had obviously got the names confused, but, said the Inspector, a glance at the register would have shown him his mistake.

At the inquiry the LMS Railway announced that it was changing all distant signals on important routes to colour lights as they fell due for renewal, thus ending the need for fogmen.

The accident, as I have said, took place at 8.18 am. At 8.30 am, prompt to time, Patten resumed duty.

11
Bourne End

(London Midland & Scottish Railway)

Of all the disasters recorded in this book Bourne End is, in a sense, the most inexplicable. A driver, forewarned by the working notices that he was to be diverted at this point, in clear daylight, disregarded two successive signal indications to reduce speed. He was a man, too, well known for his conscientious study of the notices. The Inspecting Officer thought that fatigue might have played its part, and this seems the only reasonable explanation.

Like Quintinshill, Bourne End was a case of death in the sunshine. It was a resplendent autumn Sunday morning without wind or cloud; the date was 30 September 1945. The fighting was over but trains were still vast, slow and unpunctual. So it was with the night express from Perth. The story begins at Crewe at 5 am where Royal Scot class 4–6–0 no. 6157, 'The Royal Artilleryman' was waiting on the engine siding to take the Perth train forward to London. In charge was Driver Swaby, a man of fifty-five with sixteen years' driving experience. He was in the top link at Crewe and knew the London road intimately. Swaby had booked on at 1.13 am; he had already been at work for half the night preparing his own and another engine. Take that with what we learned at Shrewsbury about drowsiness on the footplate and perhaps we have the clue to the disaster.

Swaby and his fireman, Jones, had a long wait as the express was running eighty minutes late. True to form, the driver was filling in the time by studying in detail the fortnightly notices that told of trackwork and attendant speed restrictions and diversions. From these he learned of the crossover that would occur to the slow line at Bourne End due to repairs in Watford tunnel. The train finally left Crewe at 5.45. It consisted of fifteen vehicles and carried 398 passengers.

By the time it reached Berkhamsted, just after 9 am, it was running two hours behind schedule, but catching up a bit as it touched 60 mph on the first part of the long descent to London. The Berkhamsted signalman caught sight of Swaby and Jones – a straight parallel with Grantham – and noticed each was in his place.

Bourne End (not to be confused with the station of that name in Buckinghamshire) was a half-way signal box between Berkhamsted and Hemel Hempstead. The latter station was then called Boxmoor. The distant signals were colour lights but the home ones were semaphore, with the inner home consisting of splitting signals for the junction between fast and slow tracks. Unlike the meaning where continuous colour light signalling is installed, the use of two yellows on such signals in a set-up like that at Bourne End was specifically to warn of the crossover ahead. Why Swaby failed to heed it will never be known, for both he and his fireman died instantly in the crash. Even stranger was his failure to take any action on approaching the inner home signal which clearly indicated the diversion ahead, but the evidence showed that the earliest point at which the brake was applied, if indeed it ever was, could not have been before they were practically on the points. No. 6157 was not severely damaged in the accident and was found to be in first-class working order. The regulator was still open.

As the crossover deflected the locomotive left-wards, it rolled to the right, then recovered and lurched heavily to the left, pushing the rails out of position in front of it. It reached the slow line still travelling at fully 50 mph, continued for a short distance and then turned over to the left. On both sides of this point the line is in a cutting, but just here, by unhappy chance, a short embankment intervenes. The engine dropped into a field nine feet below and slid on its side for over twenty yards, dragging six of the first seven coaches after it. They piled up into a vast heap of wreckage rising thirty feet above the engine. Perversely the second vehicle, an all steel van, stayed on the top and was thrown on its side across three tracks, little damaged. Only the last three coaches kept the rails unharmed.

Including the driver and fireman, forty-three people died in this disaster, of whom five died later in hospital. The list of the seriously injured was exceptionally high; sixty-four were in hospital for over a week.

The Inspecting Officer, Lt–Col Sir Alan

23. Bourne End. The uppermost of the heap of six carriages piled on top of their engine in the field. Onlookers and workers stand among the cabbages into which the train plunged. (*H. C. Casserley*)

24. Bourne End. A down train waits to pass the wreck of the up Perth express. The enormous height of the heap of coaches is emphasised here by the end of the uppermost vehicle seen in the previous picture. Bear in mind that the bottom of the heap is nine feet below the line where the engine lies on its side. Note the presence of the WRVS dispensing tea by the cab of the crane. These splendid women have always been in evidence at major accidents since the organisation's inception and are one of the few cheering sights at such scenes. (*H. C. Casserley*)

Mount, concluded that it was useless to speculate on the causes of Swaby's lapse. But he did comment on the fact that the driver had done twenty-six days' continuous duty, including four Sundays. Once again he urged the need for some form of automatic train control, but it needed an even more terrible disaster before the railway management was at last galvanised into action.

Since the ambiguity of the double yellow distant usage could conceivably have been a contributive cause, the Inspector suggested that its use be standardised to mean one thing only: one yellow at the next light. If used in conjunction with semaphore signals it should therefore be as an outer distant, with an inner distant showing a single yellow. As to the position of stop signals, clearance should be retarded in the case of a slow-speed diversion on a fast route to bring the speed down to safety level.

The site of the accident wants searching for now. It took a tramp of several miles along Hertfordshire lanes and a little discreet trespassing before I managed to locate it. For Bourne End has been wiped off the railway map. Signal box, crossovers, signals – all have gone; the continuous colour lights, controlled from Watford, wink beneath the catenary. A new crossover has been laid one and a half miles away near Hemel Hempstead, and there is not even a trace to mark the site of the box. Progress has finally swept it away by design, just as the Perth express almost did by accident on that brilliant Sunday morning in the autumn of 1945.

25. Bourne End. With the carriages removed, the
mutilated hulk of no. 6157, 'The Royal Artilleryman',
having been righted, is lifted out of the field – a difficult
and delicate task for the crane-crew. 'The Royal Scot' is a
sad contrast to the Class 5 locomotive heading the
recovery train behind. (*H. C. Casserley*)

12
Lichfield

(London Midland & Scottish Railway)

The collision at Lichfield Trent Valley station on the evening of New Year's Day 1946 falls into the rare class of unique accidents. A handful of ballast interfered with the working of a set of points. Although other factors were involved, it was the movement of the ballast which precipitated the accident.

Lichfield was remarkable for another reason. Time and again we have had to record how railwaymen have managed to mis-see something; but so far the men concerned have been interested parties, who may unconsciously have bent the facts in their own favour. At Lichfield, however, three quite independent witnesses – not involved in the accident in any way – were

prepared to testify that red was green. Interrogated separately four times by three different sets of people, they stuck to their story. That is a circumstance without parallel.

The diagram shows the layout of the up lines. Note the connection from the fast to the slow line controlled by No. 1 box. The numbers are those of relevant levers, with 32 actuating the locking bolt for 33. Since this bolt played a key part in the accident I had better explain its function. All facing points must be locked in position, which is done by means of a bolt which engages in a notch in the stretcher joining the two tongues of the points. The bolt is worked by a separate lever, which when pulled engages it in

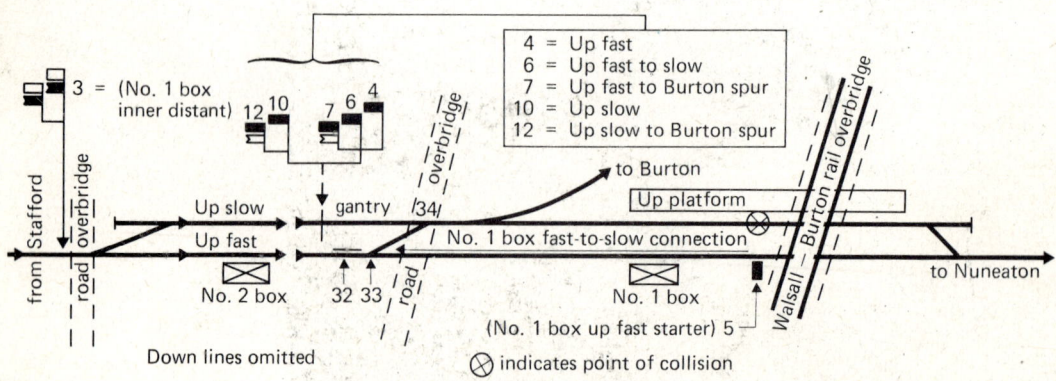

4 = Up fast
6 = Up fast to slow
7 = Up fast to Burton spur
10 = Up slow
12 = Up slow to Burton spur

⊗ indicates point of collision

Down lines omitted

Figure 5. Lichfield: track layout

the notch. This lever is normally kept in the reversed position. When the points are to be moved it must be restored to normal in order to free them, after which it is reversed again to restore the lock.

The first day of January had a fine clear evening with a few degrees of frost. The 6.08 pm slow train from Stafford to Nuneaton, a short four-coach train hauled by Prince of Wales class 4–6–0 no. 25802, had run into Lichfield station at 6.52 over the No. 1 box connection. Normally the other connection was used, but the slow line between the two was occupied by a goods train waiting to go forward along the Burton spur.

Close behind the slow was the 2.50 pm express fish train from Fleetwood to Broad Street, another short train of seven fish vans and a brake van hauled by Stanier class 5 4–6–0 no. 5495. It was due to pass the slow train at Lichfield and had been on the other's heels ever since Stafford suffering check after check.

At 6.46 Signalman Williams in No. 1 box had set the points for the local. At 6.52, having sent 'Train Out Of Section' to No. 2 box, he re-set the road for the fish train. At least he thought he had done so, but in those six minutes the ballast had moved, either forced up by the frost or by the movement of trains, or both. The effect was to impede the movement of the locking bolt mechanism, so that as Williams restored no. 32 locking bolt lever to normal the bolt itself was not quite free of the notch. He then restored lever 33 to normal for the fish train, but the points were still held locked by the bolt. So the

26. Lichfield. A newspaper picture, taken in the floodlights erected on the night of the accident, showing Stanier Class 5 4–6–0 no. 5495 surrounded by the telescoped remains of the last coach of the Stafford to Nuneaton train. The coach's left-hand sole bar is clearly visible along the length of the engine. (*Illustrated London News*)

lever moved but the points did not, i.e. they were still set for the connection to the slow line. It may seem extraordinary that the lever could thus be moved against the resistance of the rodding, but, without knowing it, Williams had bent the vertical down-rod leading from the lever to the rodding on the ground. The rest of the movement had been taken up by the springing in the rodding. Although Williams was a small man weighing only nine and a half stone, the movement had required no special effort which might have warned him that something was wrong.

The return of lever 33 to normal freed the interlocking, and Williams was able to pull off his signals for the fish train. The signal that matters is the home signal, lever no. 4, which protected the connection. On the same gantry was signal no. 6, fast to slow, also a rarely used signal no. 7, fast to Burton spur. Williams pulled no. 4 with the other fast line signals and assumed that it was off. He thought he had looked to make sure that the back light was obscured as it should have been, but was not certain of this. In any case he had no cause to doubt that the signal had been correctly pulled off, though in fact it had not been. The points had remained set for the connection and a device known as a detector, an additional safeguard to interlocking, prevented the signal being pulled off in conflict with the setting of the points. Since the detector was found afterwards to be in perfect order there could be no doubt that no. 4 had remained at danger; when Williams had pulled the lever he had merely stretched the wire, but he was now free to pull off both outer and inner distants.

Driver Read of the fish train, tired of the incessant delays, welcomed the sight of the outer distant colour light at green. 'We are going to get a clear road at last,' he remarked to his fireman, Beckett. The inner distant was also at clear, and so, Read confidently affirmed afterwards, was

the home semaphore signal – no. 4. He told the inquiry he was quite certain that it was the right hand of the three signals which was at clear. The next moment the engine gave a violent lurch as it was deflected over the connection, throwing Read into the middle of the cab. He had no idea what had happened, but had the presence of mind to shut off steam and apply the brake before striking the rear of the stationary slow train.

The slow train was standing with the brakes on, but none the less it was driven forward for nearly 100 yards, the engine ending up in the sand drag at the end of the slow line. The last three coaches of the train were wrecked and the leading coach driven into the tender and badly damaged. The fish train came to rest some 130 yards beyond the point of impact. No. 5495 had driven right through the rearmost coach, whose roof and body sides were found abreast of the tender, with the sole bars splayed out on either side of the engine. Half the second coach was found on the station platform. Thirteen passengers were killed outright and another seven died in hospital or on the way, a total of twenty. Twenty-one more were officially recorded as injured, though few can have escaped unharmed. None of the enginemen suffered serious injury, but Driver Read had to be taken to hospital with severe shock. Luckiest escape was that of the slow train guard, who was having a cup of tea in the buffet.

After the accident Fireman Beckett of the fish train came into the box. A highly mystified Williams, who took him for the driver, assured him that all the signals had been cleared for his train. The guard of the fish train, Freeman, also came into the box, and was likewise assured.

As I have said, it was not only Driver Read who was convinced that no. 4 signal was at clear. The three independent witnesses who supported him were the driver and guard of the waiting goods train and the signalman in No. 2 box, all

27. Lichfield. The scene the next day, in which the rest of the passenger train's wreckage can be seen. On the platform is half of the second carriage where it was thrown by the force of the impact. The rest of this strange dichotomy lies disintegrated along with the remains of the third coach just beyond. The train's engine, Prince of Wales class 4–6–0 no. 25802, can be seen in front of the overbridge, still upright although stuck in the sand drag at the end of the slow line. (*Illustrated London News*)

of whom were well placed to see the signal.

It was established that none of these three could have had any conversation with Driver Read, who had been taken to hospital directly after the accident. They had been questioned, separately, a few hours after the accident, then again at the Company's inquiry, then twice by the Inspecting Officer, and their accounts were the same in each case.

Here was a poser for the Inspecting Officer, faced, as he put it, with this incompatibility between the oral and the tangible evidence. However, having exhausted every possibility, he was forced to the conclusion that no. 4 signal could not have been at clear. What had happened, the Inspector thought, was this: Williams had told Beckett, the fireman of the fish train, that all the signals on the up fast line had been cleared. That started a chain of suggestion. Beckett, it was discovered, had passed the information to Guard Freeman, although he had

already heard it from Williams himself. Freeman had then gone to the station and seen Harley, the fireman of the goods train, to whom he passed on the information. Harley passed it onto his driver, Kendall, who in turn passed it onto Guard Moors. As for the man in No. 2 box, Shone, Williams when he phoned would undoubtedly have told him that everything had been in order. None of these witnesses had any special interest in the position of the signals. Several trains had passed on the up fast line during the previous hour, so all three had seen no. 4 signal at clear more than once. When they were told that it had been at clear for the fish train, this caused them to relate the information to what they had seen earlier, with identical inaccurate results.

A study of railway accidents is an education in the human capacity for self-deception. The Lichfield accident is surely the classic example.

13
Goswick

(London and North Eastern Railway)

The last months of independent railways in Britain were marked by two serious accidents at opposite ends of the country, and they occurred within only two days of each other. The first involved a couple of Southern Electric trains at South Croydon in the outer London suburbs. It was the worst crash in the company's history and a sad end to the old SR. The other, the last great accident before all was swept into the maw of British Railways, was on the LNER at Goswick in Northumberland on 26 October 1947. In many ways it was another Bourne End. An express, due to be diverted for Sunday engineering work, disregarded the warning signals in clear daylight, took the turnout at a high speed and was derailed on a low embankment. In this case, however, the driver and fireman lived to tell the tale, which from their point of view was not a creditable one. For that reason I shall not mention their names.

There was a third party on the footplate: an engine-crazy naval rating who had talked the driver into giving him a ride. Whether the presence of this illicit passenger had any bearing on the accident is uncertain, but it may have done.

Goswick, now closed, was a wayside station on the East Coast main line about seven miles south of Berwick. On this Sunday, because of bridge repairs, all traffic was being diverted onto goods train running-loops, known here for some reason as the 'independent lines'. The work, which was due to finish by one o'clock, had been postponed from the previous weekend. The weather, in stark contrast to the fog which had shrouded South Croydon two days earlier, was bright and clear, with a south-easterly breeze blowing off the North Sea.

The up signals at Goswick consisted of a distant placed far out (1,647 yards) from the home signal, doubtless on account of the falling gradient; the home signal 268 yards from the box, and splitting starters – main line, main-to-independent – close to the box itself. Signalman White, having had word that the engineer's gang was ready to start, set the road for the up independent line, bolted the points and put a collar on the lever. With the points set thus the distant signal was locked at caution and the up main starter at danger. The home signal and main-to-independent starter remained free of the interlocking.

The scene shifts to the Haymarket engine-shed in Edinburgh. The driver was going in by the back entrance to avoid being seen, for he had his unauthorised guest with him. This was the naval rating, who was wearing overalls borrowed from his fireman brother so as not to attract attention. When he had dispatched his

28. Goswick. A3 Pacific no. 66, 'Merry Hampton', lies canted in the ditch while casualties are passed out of one of the wrecked carriages. (*Illustrated London News*)

guest to the engine, the driver proceeded to sign on and study the notices. He overlooked the pencilled sheet on the late notices board that told of the re-scheduled bridge work. So he set off from the shed unaware that he was to be diverted at Goswick. The fireman was also unaware, as he had turned up late and had had no time to look at the board. Even the guard was unaware. In the guards' room at Waverley station all the late notices, including a number of old ones, were clipped together on a badly illuminated board. The man looked through them, but managed to miss the crucial one. So no one on the train knew of the diversion. This would not have mattered, of course, had the driver observed the signals.

Their train was the day Scotsman which left Waverley at 11.15 am in the charge of A3 Pacific no. 66, 'Merry Hampton'. It consisted of fifteen coaches with 420 passengers aboard – almost exactly the same as the Perth express at Bourne End.

Just ninety minutes later, at 12.45, Signalman White received 'Train Entering Section' for the Scotsman from Scremerston, the next box to the north. He held his home signal at danger, intending to see the train come nearly to a standstill before pulling it off – thus ensuring that the change of track would be taken at a safe speed. 'Merry Hampton' first came into sight as it passed through an overbridge 1,457 yards from the box, a quarter of a mile beyond the distant, by which time it ought to have shut off steam. White had an almost direct head-on view of the train, which made it difficult for him to gauge its speed accurately. He saw some steam, but supposed it to be coming from the safety valve after the regulator had been closed. Assuming

29. Goswick. In this aerial view of the scene, the engine is in the centre of the left hand side. Just how bad the consequences would have been with inferior rolling-stock and fewer, if any, buck-eye couplings, makes for horrific speculation in view of the damage caused even with these advantages. That only twenty-eight died out of the 420 aboard seems little short of a miracle. (*Illustrated London News*)

the train was slowing down, he allowed it to approach to within 360 yards of the home signal, which he then pulled off. He kept the starter at danger. As the express was coming up to the home signal, White realised it was still steaming and travelling fast. He threw the signal back to danger just before the engine reached it and used the emergency remote-controlled detonator-placer. He then stood at the window and waved his arms frantically. The driver appeared to have shut off steam when he passed, but the brakes did not appear to have been applied.

That was White's account. The driver's was different. He missed the distant, he said, because of steam blowing down onto the cab window. This may well have been the case as the Pacifics were driven from the right and a south-easterly wind would blow the exhaust to that side close to the engine. He put on the blower to try and clear it, but to no avail. He did not explain why he did not move across to the other side of the cab to observe the distant, or ask his fireman to look out for it. Having missed the signal, he claimed, he shut off steam, but a moment later got a sight of the home signal showing clear and did not, therefore, apply the brakes.

Not surprisingly, the Inspector accepted White's account. How much of the driver's story was genuine self-deception and how much plain lies we shall never know.

So 'Merry Hampton' took the facing points unchecked at a speed of at least 60 mph. Turnouts onto goods lines are not laid out to be taken at any but the slowest speeds; this one had a two-inch wrong way cant owing to the curvature of the main line and could not be negotiated safely at anything more than 15–20 mph. The engine turned over into the ditch with its wheels spinning, and eight of the leading nine vehicles followed it.

At Bourne End much of the death-toll was attributed to the telescoping of the carriages. At Goswick, however, the combination of buck-eye couplings, which were fitted to most of the coaches, and the superior construction of the Pullman vestibule stock prevented a recurrence. In the earlier accident it may be recalled that forty-three died and many more were seriously injured. At Goswick, with a similar load, the toll was significantly lower at twenty-eight dead and far fewer seriously hurt. We may give the couplings, all of which held, much of the credit for the less tragic figures, bad though they were.

The poor sailor, like the other two on the footplate, survived but was badly hurt. He paid highly for his eagerly sought trip and doubtless forfeited for ever the prospect of a career among his beloved engines.

14
Winsford

(London Midland Region, BR)

This might be called the story of the soldier who wanted his wife, or of the signalman who wanted his supper. It happened about half an hour after midnight on 17 April 1948; it was the newly formed British Railways' first big accident.

Travelling in the 5.40 pm express from Glasgow was an artilleryman aged nineteen, married and irresponsible. He was an ex-railwayman who before joining up had worked in Winsford Junction box, which he was just passing. He was on leave, in love and less than a mile from home – his in-laws' home, to be exact. Why be carried on to Crewe, he reasoned, eight miles further on, and have to wait until seven o'clock next morning for a train back, when there was a perfectly good communication cord? So he went into the toilet and pulled it, and when the train had come to a standstill he slipped away across the moonlit fields. As a former railway-man he knew how a standing train was protected, and so of course should this train have been. As it was, he bought the extra night with his wife at a cost of twenty-four lives. It is to his credit that after the accident he came forward and owned up.

As soon as the train had stopped, the fireman, Price, got down from the footplate of Princess Pacific no. 6207, 'Princess Arthur of Con-

naught', and began to walk back along the train, examining the coach ends for the turned disc marking the coach in which the cord had been pulled. The guard meanwhile had been walking up the other way, examining the vacuum pipe and generally trying to find out what was amiss. I shall call the guard Sandy; he was sixty-three and he appears as a well-meaning and rather clumsy figure, with an unbelievably broad Scottish accent. A train making an emergency stop has to be protected without delay, which is the guard's duty except in one circumstance. This is when the communication cord has been pulled. Then the guard must seek out the passenger who pulled it and find out what he wants, while the fireman goes back to protect the train. This consists of laying detonators at stated intervals and displaying a hand signal – at night, a red lamp. However, Sandy in his wisdom decided that he was the more experienced man to go back. He told Price to continue looking for the coach, while he returned to his van for detonators and set off to the rear. It might have been better if he and Price had stuck to their prescribed tasks, for he managed to trip over a sleeper and his lamp went out. All this had taken a good deal longer than he realised, and having to re-light his lamp made it longer still. In fact the express had been standing for seventeen minutes, and there was another train following behind. Sandy had only had time to go about 400 yards and lay a couple of detonators before the following train was upon him.

This was the up Glasgow Postal, running late. It should have passed the express at Lancaster, but the latter had been allowed to go forward. Driver Howie, in charge of Pacific no. 6251, 'City of Nottingham', was making up time along the level track, probably doing nearer 70 than 60 mph. He had passed Winsford Junction under clear signals when he saw a red light being waved by the track and heard the crack of a detonator. He immediately shut off steam and applied the brakes – we observe some quick action here – but could only bring down his speed to about 45 mph before he crashed into the rear of the stationary express.

Let us look at what had been happening in the signal boxes. At Winsford Junction was Signalman Chamberlain, a man of sixty-six and old to be still at work, but he was fully alert. He had sent 'Train Entering Section' to Winsford Station box for the express as it had passed his

30. Winsford. Duchess Pacific no. 6251, 'City of Nottingham' lies with steam still rising in the middle of the two wrecked trains. Its leading coach, which was a GWR milk van – an odd component of a postal train – stands behind the tender surprisingly intact but little else of the train remains identifiable. Between the carriage in the foreground and the locomotive is all that is left of the two vehicles in which the passenger deaths occurred. (*Illustrated London News*)

31. Winsford. 'City of Nottingham' later on in the clearing-up operations. Little more than the bogies are left of the coach it struck at 45 mph and telescoped into matchwood. (*Illustrated London News*)

box at 12.09 am, and on this short block section he had expected the 'Train Out Of Section' signal a minute or two later – but no signal came. After five minutes, at 12.14, he had phoned the man at Winsford Station, who plays the principal part in this story and whom I shall call Harris. Harris had replied that he had missed the tail lamp, as a goods train passing in the other direction had blocked his view. This had seemed odd to Chamberlain, as the goods in question had already reached Winsford Junction and must have passed Winsford station some minutes before the express could have got there. However, he had supposed that Harris, having missed the tail lamp, was 'holding the block' as required by the rules and was waiting to get

clearance from Minshull Vernon, the next box ahead, before clearing back to Winsford Junction. When Harris sent 'Train Out Of Section' at 12.17, Chamberlain had been entirely satisfied. At 12.22 he had offered the Postal to Harris, who had accepted it at once. It had passed the box at 12.16 and a minute or so later Chamberlain heard a dull thud. He thought no more of it until he saw a red light approaching along the line, and Sandy entered in a state of high emotion, but Chamberlain could hardly understand a word of the man's thick brogue. It appeared that something dreadful had happened, but it was only when Guard Horne of the Postal reached the box ten minutes later that Chamberlain realised there had been a collision. Horne distinguished himself on this night. He had been thrown to the floor and received chest injuries, but he had made his way to the box and afterwards returned to the accident where he set a passenger's broken arm before being treated himself.

We move to Winsford Station box and meet Harris, another elderly man of sixty-two. A signalman was prone to the occupational hazards of hernia and indigestion – the first due to stiff levers and the second to having to bolt his meals between passing trains. Harris had had a hernia operation three years earlier, and we may suspect that he was liable to indigestion. That seems the most likely reason for his pre-occupation with his midnight hot supper, for his box remarkably contained a cooking stove. At this time too he was under the weather with a cold, and he had been anxious about his wife's health. All this adds up to a man more than usually liable to commit an error.

At the time when 'Train Entering Section' was given from Winsford Junction, Harris had been about to take his meal from the oven and the kettle was boiling. His mind had been more on his supper than on the train, so two minutes later, by which time the express should have passed, he assumed that it had actually done so. We know this because he had entered it in his register at that time and had sent the 'Train Entering Section' at the same time to Minshull Vernon. It should be said in his favour, however, that he admitted he was responsible for the accident.

Meanwhile, at Minshull Vernon, Signalman Morris had been wondering what had happened to the express. He had thought it might have been checked in Winsford station, so at 12.16 he had phoned Harris to ask if it was 'doing all right'. Harris had replied: 'Yes.' Morris had left his box and looked along the line, and as he could see no train he had taken the precaution of stopping the down Postal, which was approaching his box at that moment, and of cautioning the driver. This procedure is required by the regulations when a train has been an unusually long time in a section, and by carrying it out Morris prevented a double collision of the Quintinshill pattern.

Thus Harris had been reminded twice, by Chamberlain's call at 12.14 and by Morris's two minutes later. Possibly shaken in his belief by these calls, he had gone down onto the line, but seeing nothing – the standing express was hidden from his view by an overbridge – his conviction had re-asserted itself, and he had cleared back at 12.17 as has been described. Five minutes later he had accepted the Postal.

We return to the scene of the collision. When Price and his driver had at last located and restored the turned disc, the train's brakes came off. The shock of the impact was thus to that extent lessened, but the 45 mph crunch turned the rear coach into a mass of wreckage, which telescoped the rear part of the coach in front. All the dead were in these two coaches; beyond that there was little damage. The shock wave broke the couplings behind the sixth coach, an action which applied the brake again by severing the pipe. On the Postal train the second, third and fourth vehicles were badly telescoped, but the leading vehicle was, freakishly, but little damaged.

When the line was electrified a little over a decade later, full colour-light signalling and continuous track-circuiting were installed. This, together with automatic train control, would certainly prevent a rear collision happening here again. Or would it? On Boxing Day 1962 a diesel-hauled express ran into the rear of an electric one, only two miles further down the line, and eighteen died. All the sophisticated, modern equipment had been defeated by human error – in that case a crass one made by the diesel driver who misapplied a safety rule. Winsford was to join that select and sombre list of places with two railway disasters to their names.

15
Harrow

(London Midland Region, BR)

It happened on 8 October 1952 at 8.18½ am. We know the time so exactly because the shock of the collision stopped all the clocks at Harrow and Wealdstone station. Even among great disasters Harrow holds a special place. It shares two distinctions with Quintinshill: it was a double collision, and it is the only other British railway accident in which the number of dead ran into three figures. Even so it fails to challenge that ultimate horror, for, though 112 lives were lost, the terrible total was less than half that at Quintinshill.

Fifteen miles down the line from Harrow is Bourne End, where the Perth–Euston sleeping-car express crashed in 1945. The same service, reduced now from fifteen to eleven vehicles and carrying only eighty-five passengers – indicative of the decline in rail travel – was one of the trains involved at Harrow. On this calm autumn morning it was hauled by Duchess Pacific no. 46242, 'City of Glasgow'. Its driver was forty-three year old Jones of Crewe North shed, where he was known as 'a methodical young man'. His fireman, Turnock, was twenty-three and a keen, steady type, 'out to build himself up to be a good driver'.

Approaching Harrow from the other direction, fairly well filled with about 200 passengers, was the 8 am express from Euston to Liverpool

and Manchester, consisting of fifteen vehicles double-headed by Jubilee 4–6–0 no. 45637, 'Windward Islands' and, as train engine, Princess Pacific no. 46202, 'Princess Anne'.

The Perth express had been having a bad run. From Wigan southwards it had been travelling through continuous fog. Already thirty-two minutes late leaving Crewe, the train was now eighty minutes behind time, but as it approached London the fog began to grow less dense. By the time Harrow was reached, visibility had risen to between 100 and 300 yards – not enough to interfere seriously with the observation of signals.

We now join Signalman Armitage in Harrow No. 1 box, on the country side of Harrow station and controlling the crossover there. Armitage was aged thirty-four, and his first box on re-joining the railway after leaving the Army had been, strangely enough, Bourne End. He was now a relief signalman covering a number of boxes – a responsible position, for the relief man must be familiar with the working of them all. He was described as sensitive, and was badly shocked by the spectacle of the collision, but he showed that he knew how to act like a good signalman. When he had come on duty at six o'clock his 'fog object' – the back light of his home signal 303 yards distant – had been visible,

32. Harrow. In the foreground Jubilee 4–6–0 no. 45637, 'Windward Islands', lies in front of Princess Pacific no. 46202, 'Princess Anne', where they landed on the electric tracks after leaping the platform at the head of the Liverpool-bound train. 'Princess Anne' had spent most of its career converted experimentally to non-condensing turbine drive. The experiment had not been sufficiently successful to justify continuing so the engine had been converted back to conventional form a few months before this, its last journey. (Fox)

but by 6.35 it had been obscured, and since no fogman was available he had resorted to fog working (as described in the Eccles chapter). At 8.10, however, the sun was beginning to break through; he could see his 'fog object' again and resumed normal working.

Approaching on the up slow line was the 7.31 local from Tring, hauled by class 4 2–6–4T no. 42389 running bunker first. Owing to the fog it was about five minutes behind time. It was scheduled to cross over the fast line at Harrow, in order to leave the up slow line clear for the morning procession of empty stock movements into Euston from Stonebridge Park sidings. All railway managements give high priority to the punctuality of their suburban services, so the orders were to give these trains precedence over any night express that might be running late, even if it meant delaying the latter by a further two or three minutes. The local was therefore to cross over in front of the express.

79

33. Harrow. On the right is United States Air Force nurse, Abbie Sweetwine, from Florida who worked tirelessly for hours giving blood transfusions, administering morphia and comforting the injured. Here she is seen holding plasma at the first aid post set up on platform 6 while a British soldier is tended by other United States Air Force medical staff. (*Fox*)

Armitage accepted the local from Hatch End on the slow line at 8.07, and at 8.11 he accepted the Perth express on the fast line up to his outer home signal, as he was entitled to do under normal working. (If it had been one minute earlier, when fog working was still in force, he would not have been able to accept it at all.) He received 'Train Entering Section' for the local at 8.14, and after a goods train had passed his box on the down slow line he reversed the points for the crossover.

The local duly crossed over to the fast line and came to a stop in Harrow station at 8.17.

The Liverpool train had been late leaving Euston, but was making up time, and was mounting the 1 in 339 gradient at much the same speed as the Perth train was approaching down-hill, namely 55–60 mph. Armitage received 'Train Entering Section' for both trains at 8.17. About a minute later he was astonished to hear the Perth express approaching at speed; then it came out of the mist by the outer home signal, making no attempt to stop. With only seconds available, Armitage gave a copy-book demon-stration of how a signalman should act in an emergency. He pulled his lever to place a detonator on the line in the path of the Perth train and threw his signals to danger in front of the Liverpool train. But at that moment the annunciator buzzer sounded in the box, show-ing that the Liverpool train had reached the track circuit in rear of the home signal, just at the south end of the station platform. His efforts had been in vain.

Armitage was now the compulsory witness of a scene only rivalled by that observed by the guilty pair at Quintinshill. No wonder after the accident the stationmaster found him deathly white. The two collisions were practically simultaneous. The Perth train had hardly

34. Harrow. With night falling on the day of the disaster, oxy-acetylene equipment is used to cut away some of the more solid wreckage while firemen stand by against the always present danger. (*Radio Times Hulton Picture Library*)

on account of track and signalling work at Euston. It contained about 800 passengers, that is about eleven to a compartment, and was preparing to depart when those in the front felt three heavy shocks as the Perth train destroyed the rear three coaches in succession. The local was standing with its brakes off, but was only driven forward about an engine's length.

'City of Glasgow', on the Perth express, was deflected to the right and came to rest on its right side on the down main line, directly in the path of the Liverpool train which was bearing down on it at high speed. The Jubilee at the head of the latter struck it full on. The crunch between a 700-ton fast-moving mass and a 100-ton obstacle produced destruction on a spectacular scale. The Jubilee was thrown to the left clean across the platform, where it swept to their death passengers waiting for the next electric train. It landed on its side across the electric lines, a complete ruin. It was followed by 'Princess Anne', likewise shattered, though the crew survived. Not even modern stock could withstand the force of such a collision. Sixteen vehicles were destroyed or practically so – five in the Perth train, three in the local and eight in the Liverpool train. Thirteen of these were piled into a heap of wreckage forty feet high, burying 'City of Glasgow' and its dead crew. One corner of the pile struck the footbridge spanning the platforms and brought down a girder to add to the wreck. The driver of the leading engine was killed, but the fireman had a remarkable escape. Somehow he was thrown clear, and when he came to he found himself on the upturned wheel splasher of the train engine.

Of the 108 passengers killed it was estimated that sixty-four were in the local, twenty-three in the Perth sleeper but, astonishingly, only seven in the Liverpool train. The remaining fourteen were probably waiting on the up electric-line platform. The injured had reason to be grateful

crashed into the rear of the standing local, shattering the last three coaches, when the Liverpool train ploughed into the wreckage.

The local was more than usually full, for another train had been cancelled that morning

35. Harrow. Duchess Pacific no. 46242, 'City of Glasgow', which headed the Scottish express and ran into the back of the local, after two days of salvage efforts had uncovered it from under the forty-foot high pile of wreckage. Hardly recognisable as a locomotive any more, the front right hand driving wheel and leading bogies can be seen in the centre bottom of the picture. (*Associated Press*.)

that the American Air Force HQ was nearby at Ruislip. Its response to a call for help was magnificent. From depots and airfields over a wide area came 500 doctors and nurses with all their superb field equipment. As the *Daily Mirror* wrote: 'The injured didn't have to wait to go to hospital for treatment – the hospital came to them.' I, for one, long remember the picture of the coloured nurse from Florida, Abbie Sweetwine, cradling a badly hurt passenger while the American doctor attends him, also the Boston sergeant's comment on the behaviour of the injured: 'The British don't cry.'

To the Inspecting Officer, Lt–Col Wilson, fell the task of trying to probe the cause of the disaster. He examined a number of possibilities and came up with a suggested explanation, feasible if purely conjectural. Driver Jones, in the prevailing conditions of visibility, had possibly only four seconds in which to observe the colour light distant, though for that time it would have shone with increasing brilliance. If Jones had missed it without realising he had done so, he might have continued to look out for it at its height of fourteen feet above the ground, and thus have missed the outer and inner home semaphores, set at a height of thirty feet and more. In that case only when the surroundings of Harrow station came into view would he have realised where he was – it was established that the brakes were applied a few seconds before the crash. The fireman would have had no cause to be looking out for the signals, as they were on the left-hand – the driver's – side.

Harrow was another accident that could have been prevented by automatic train control, but British Railways were still developing a standardised system suitable for all kinds of line. A prototype had been agreed only two months before, but it was 1956 before final Ministry approval was given. Though even Automatic Warning System (as it is now officially called) did not prevent the rear-end collision at Winsford in 1962, as was noted in the previous chapter. Nor did such a system prevent one at Dagenham East in 1958. Where semaphore signalling existed, only the distants were so equipped. It was a starter signal, missed in the fog, that led to the Dagenham disaster.

The layout at Harrow was altered after the accident, and the crossover was transferred to the London end of the platform. Had this been done before, the local train would have been standing at the slow-line platform and the express would have been safely on another track. Gone now is the signal box, along with all the other station boxes on this route, the whole stretch being controlled from the new box at Willesden. That, of course, all happened when the main line was electrified. The Scottish expresses that now rush through Harrow under the catenary provide another link with the only worse disaster on Britain's railways. For just four hours or so down the line is Quintinshill.

16

Lewisham

(Southern Region, BR)

Our story opens at Cannon Street shortly before six o'clock on the evening of 4 December 1957. Driver Trew and Fireman Hoare, of Ramsgate, had been shivering for over an hour on the fogbound and freezing platform waiting for their much delayed train to be hauled in. This was the 4.56 pm to Ramsgate via Folkestone – in effect the same train as the one that had been derailed at Sevenoaks thirty years before. It was five minutes to six before Trew and Hoare were at last able to board their engine, Battle of Britain class light Pacific no. 34066, 'Spitfire'.

I should not have liked to be in Trew's place. The Battle of Britain Pacifics, like the larger Merchant Navy class, were fitted with side sheets to the boiler, for no better reason than that their designer considered it gave them a 'modern' look. Some of both classes had been rebuilt without the side sheets, but 'Spitfire' was not one of them. These sheets obstructed the look-out, which was further restricted by a narrow 8' 6" cab to enable the engines to work through the Bo-peep tunnel on the Hastings line. To have charge of such an engine on a foggy night must in itself have been no small strain.

The 4.56 finally got away at 6.08 pm, seventy-two minutes late, overfilled with 700 passengers who had accumulated during the long wait. For the first three and a half miles to New Cross all went well. The line is continuously on viaduct and the fog was less dense than at ground level. Each successive colour light showed green, and Trew was able to keep going at 30–35 mph. The light at the far end of New Cross platform, A42, was likewise at green. Then suddenly, without warning, as is the way with fog at night, the train plunged into the opaque blackness of the cutting beyond.

We must now see what was happening just over a mile further on at Parks Bridge Junction, where the mid-Kent line for Hayes and Addiscombe diverges to the right from the main line. Halted at the junction lights was the 5.25 pm Charing Cross to Hastings diesel, and halted at the previous light, 476 yards in rear, was the 5.18 pm electric train from Charing Cross to Hayes, its ten coaches crammed to bursting with 1,500 passengers. As the times show, these trains were running in their wrong order owing to the fog. The Hastings train need not have been stopped, but Signalman Beckett at Parks Bridge was under the impression that it was the Hayes train, and had therefore halted it to allow a train on the up main line to pass. The reasons for the misunderstanding are worth explaining, because they are a perfect example of how small circumstances can lead to great disasters. The Hastings service had only lately been dieselised, and there was no separate space on the 'describer' (the box-to-box route indicator) to distinguish it from a main line electric. Such a train – to Orpington – had just passed, and Beckett had missed the next – identical – 'description' from St Johns for the Hastings run. Thus it was he came to believe that it was the Hayes train standing at his signals, and a phone call to the box from the Hastings driver did not remove his misapprehension; perhaps the Hayes driver also phoned at just about the same time. Probably the mistake would not have occurred if Beckett had had a booking-boy as he should have done, but boy labour was hard to come by in London. Beckett was, of course, in no sense responsible for the accident, but if he had got his trains right both the Hastings and Hayes trains would have been on their way, and there would have been no collision.

138 yards in rear of the tail of the Hayes train was colour light L18, of course showing red. Behind it, at roughly quarter-mile intervals, were lights L17 and L16, correctly showing one and two yellows respectively. Behind L16 again was the New Cross light A42, which Trew had just passed at green. All these lights were on the right-hand side, the fireman's side in this class of engine, but in clear weather L16 and L17 could first be seen by the driver because of the left-hand curve. But the long boiler with its side sheets cut off his view eighty yards away or even further, and here visibility was suddenly reduced to a mere twenty yards or so. A quick-

36. Lewisham. A picture taken on the down side of the overbridge looking towards St Johns. The second coach of the Ramsgate train lies crushed under the collapsed viaduct while the rear of the leading coach can be seen in the foreground. (Fox)

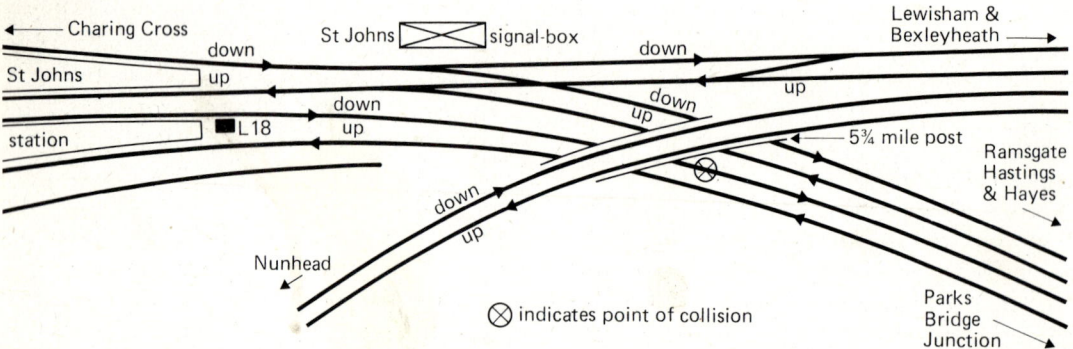

37. Lewisham. Just how devastating an effect the bridge collapse had on the second coach can be seen here after much of the debris has been removed. The still dangerous bridge has been propped up and screens erected to shield the more gruesome and tragic discoveries from the curiosity of the inevitable sightseers. (*Fox*)

Figure 6. Lewisham: track layout

thinking man might have called out to his fireman to look out for these two signals, as the driver of the preceding steam train had done, but Trew, though steady and conscientious, was no quick thinker. In this respect he differed not at all from a number of other drivers we have encountered who were not held blameworthy. His statements afterwards were confused – small wonder – but I believe that we can follow his thoughts. He had had the green at New Cross, and he had never before been checked at any of the succeeding lights, which he took for granted would be showing clear. If I read his character aright, this was not a conscious assumption, or in any sense a deliberate disregard of the lights. The possibility that they might be at caution simply did not cross his mind, or did not do so in time, and because of that he brought about the accident.

At L18 Hoare was looking out; 'Red,' he called across to Trew. With the tail of the Hayes train 138 yards ahead, instant action might still have prevented the collision or reduced its violence. The line rises at this point at 1 in 218, and calculations showed that at 30 mph the train could have been stopped in 130 yards. Trew shut off steam and applied the brake, but not quickly enough to make much difference. His train was still travelling at about 30 mph when it struck the Hayes train. The latter was standing with the brakes on to hold it on the gradient; a near-immovable 400-ton obstacle.

'Spitfire' embedded itself in the rear coach of the Hayes train, killing the guard, but it was the eighth coach that suffered most. It was over-ridden by the ninth coach and the bodywork destroyed. The damage to the Ramsgate train was still worse. The rear of the electric train was standing just ahead of an overbridge, a two-span girder affair carrying the Nunhead–Lewisham link over the main lines. The tender of the Pacific and the leading coach were flung against one of the stanchions, bringing down two of the heavy girders onto the still moving train. The second coach and half the third were crushed beneath their weight. Strange to say, 'Spitfire' kept the rails, though its front end was badly damaged.

A driver and fireman were travelling in the Hayes train and they went back to the engine and threw out the fire. They found Trew still on the footplate, unhurt but badly shocked. The fireman was severely injured.

Ninety people lost their lives, making it the third-worst disaster on our railways. It could, however, have displaced Harrow as the second-worst had it not been for the alertness and quick thinking of another train driver. Two minutes after the crash, Motorman Corke was approaching the overbridge on the elevated line with the 5.22 electric train from Holborn Viaduct. Peering ahead through the mist he noticed that the girders were tilting. Quick as thought he cut off power and braked and managed to bring his train to a standstill on the shelving track, with its leading coach actually above the mangled vehicles of the Ramsgate train. Any less prompt action would have caused the train to be precipitated onto the wreckage below.

There was a harrowing sequel for Trew. The Inspecting Officer, while bound to hold him responsible, showed an understanding of the man and the circumstances. But the Coroner's jury took a different view, and Trew found himself on a charge of manslaughter. At the first trial on 21 April the jury disagreed – it would be fascinating to know how the voting went – but at the re-trial on 8 May the Crown offered no evidence. After five months Trew's ordeal was over.

The mile post which shows that Charing Cross is exactly five and three quarter miles away marks the point at which it all so tragically happened. Two miles further down the line is Hither Green where forty-nine were to die ten

38. Lewisham. The end of the Hayes train about to be lifted free of Battle of Britain class light Pacific no. 34066, 'Spitfire', which is still rammed into it. The motor coach at the rear of the ten car electric train has survived the collision remarkably well, but the eighth coach was almost totally destroyed after being overridden by the ninth as can be glimpsed in the background. Despite this, and bearing in mind that each carriage was carrying about 150 people, the toll of thirty-seven passengers killed in the suburban train seems miraculously light. (*Central Press*)

years later when a diesel-electric train struck a broken rail. Three and three-quarter miles from St Johns through Lewisham on the Bexleyheath loop is Eltham Well Hall where, with echoes of those 'runaways' in the first chapter, a diesel-hauled excursion train failed to negotiate a 20 mph curve. The inebriated driver was doing about 65 mph and killed himself and five passengers, injuring 126 more. That was in June 1972 and completed the tragic triangle of accidents which began that foggy evening late in 1957.

17
Settle

(London Midland Region, BR)

For our final chapter we return to the spectacular Settle and Carlisle line across the Pennines. Indeed we visit first the very place where, almost exactly half a century before, Signalman Sutton had made the fatal mistake that sent the Scottish express to its destruction. Those fifty years had seen some changes at Hawes Junction; for one thing, with the line to Hawes closed, the name had changed to Garsdale after the parish in which it stood. But in the early hours of 21 January 1960, with a gale once again sweeping through a bleak black night, it would not have looked much different from that Christmas Eve in 1910 – though the snow that was being driven against the windows of the signal box would have been more appropriate then.

Driver Waites, aboard a Britannia class engine no. 70052, 'Firth of Tay' was taking the 9.05 pm train from Glasgow (St Enoch) to St Pancras. This service took the 'Midland' route via Dumfries and was booked to call not only there but also at Kilmarnock, Annan and Carlisle. It was an eight-coach affair, all modern stock with buck-eye couplings, the last three coaches being sleeping cars. A brake van brought up the rear. The schedule gave it just over four hours to reach Ais Gill box, and it was running to time when, at 1.10 am on the 21st, it passed over the

summit there. Waites notched up the reversing lever for the descent, and it was then for the first time that he noticed something was wrong. There was an ominous knocking sound coming from the front. He reduced speed by shutting the regulator, but that seemed to make the noise worse so he used the brake instead. He decided to examine the engine at the first opportunity and so made an un-scheduled stop at Garsdale, some two miles further on.

He suspected it was a big end bearing that was causing the trouble, so he felt the bearings and examined the motion as best he could, but it was a really foul night and the blizzard was blinding him with snow. Moreover he had only a small battery-torch to see by. Having failed to discover anything wrong, he climbed back onto the footplate and told his fireman, Chester, that he thought they should go on slowly to Hellifield depot, five miles beyond Settle, and have the knocking investigated there. He did not, however, send a message ahead to the Shedmaster as he should have done.

So Waites and Chester set off again, contentedly unaware that they had in fact already lost two crucial parts of the Britannia's right-hand motion assembly.

On the long falling gradient from Blea Moor, despite the intention to take it gently, their speed

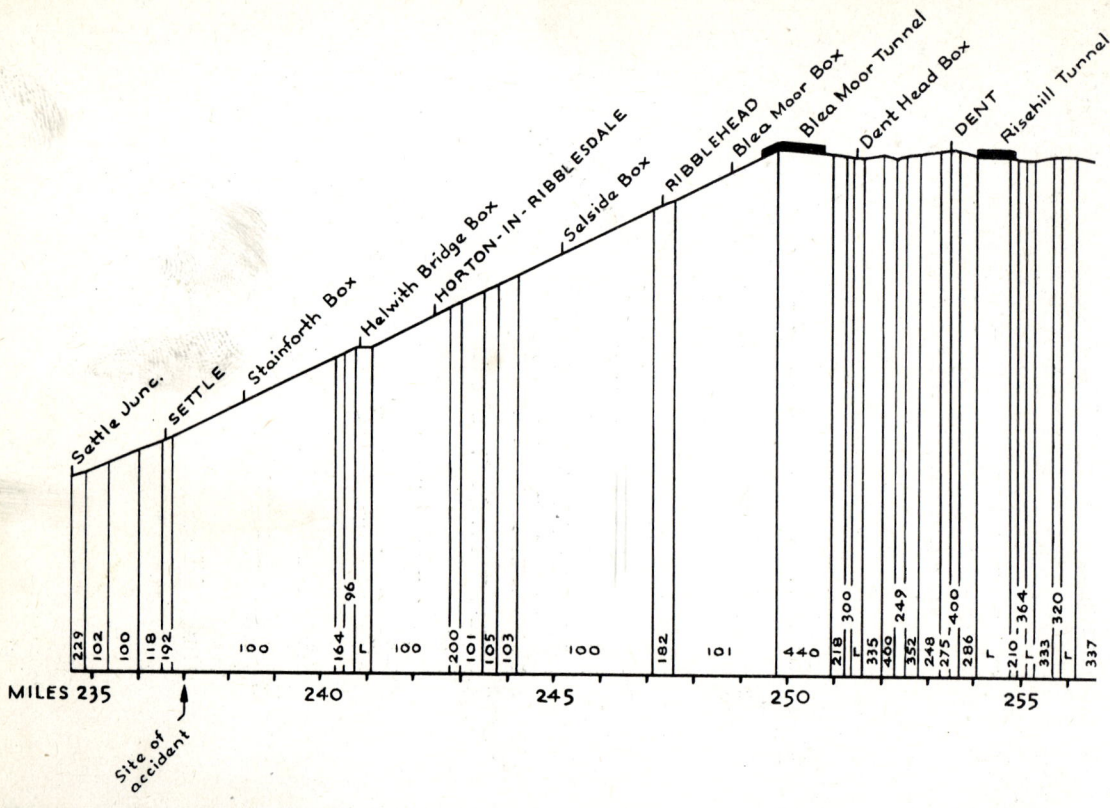

Figure 7. Settle: gradient profile of part of the Carlisle to Settle line over the Pennines, showing the places at which the various parts of the Britannia's right hand slide bars were found. The profile is also an interesting illustration of the character of this famous and spectacular stretch of railway.

gradually rose. Doubtless Waites was lulled into a false sense of security by the fact that the knocking did not seem to be getting any worse, and also he was fairly certain that it was coming from a big end as this was the usual reason for such noises from engines. They had averaged about 40 mph over the twenty miles from Garsdale when they passed the Settle distant signal. Suddenly they were startled by ballast being thrown up against the cab and simultaneously saw sparks flying up from the right-hand side. Waites threw the brakes full on but it was too late. The right-hand piston rod, cross head and

connecting rod, still attached to the driving wheel, were driven deep into the formation between the tracks and then overturned into a trailing position. Miraculously this did not thrust the engine off the rails, and all might still have been well had a freight train not been coming along the other line. The twenty-vehicle goods train was on its way to Carlisle from Leeds and was hauled by a 2–6–0 class 5 MT 'Crab' locomotive no. 42881. It was just about to pass the express when the Britannia's cross head struck the inner rail of the down line, damaging it critically. The 5 MT locomotive was derailed towards the up

90

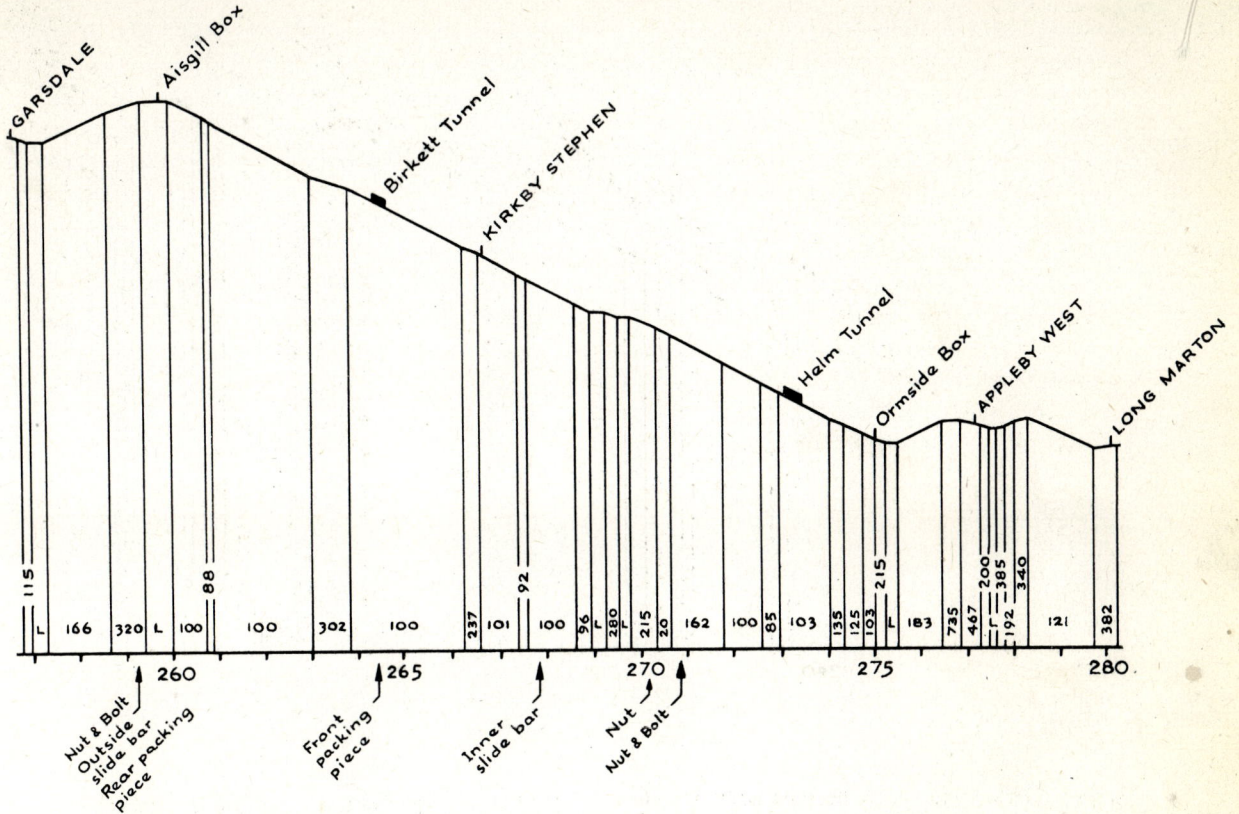

line and tore out the sides of the first three coaches of the express, badly damaging the remainder. Of the seventy-five passengers aboard, five died and eight were injured as was the guard of the freight train.

In his conclusions after the inquiry, the Inspecting Officer, Brigadier Langley, laid the bulk of the blame on the maintenance staff. The accident happened because of their failure to tighten properly the right-hand slide bar bolts and ensure the split-pins were in sound condition and bearing directly upon the nuts they were there to retain. The first nut and bolt had fallen off just after Helm Tunnel on the climb to Ais Gill, followed shortly by the bottom inner slide bar it had held. The bottom outer slide bar had gone just as the summit was passed and the vibration set up between the loose cross head and the top slide bar started the knocking sound that was heard from that point onwards. After that it was only a matter of time until the whole assembly came to grief.

The maintenance failure was all the more difficult to excuse, the inspector felt, because the tendency for these bolts to loosen was a feature of this class of engine, and the danger therefore was well known. The bolts in question, however, were difficult to reach and tighten, and this may have led to a certain laxness in attending to them. No. 70052 had a particularly poor record in respect of these bolts, with no less than nine reports of their being found loose since the engine last came out of the shops. Modification to eliminate the problem was already being carried out on the Britannias as they went in for overhaul or repair, but no. 70052 had not yet been done and no one appears to have suggested it should have had priority.

Driver Waites, whilst perhaps knowing something of these problems in general, would of course have been unlikely to know that no. 70052 was a bad case since it was only one of the various locomotives to which he was assigned. Furthermore there had been no previous instance of trouble being experienced during running. So Brigadier Langley did not criticise him for failing to diagnose the cause of the knocking correctly, nor even for failing to notice the missing parts at Garsdale. The inspector accepted that the assembly could easily have seemed all right in the appalling conditions

39. Settle. Crab 2–6–0 freight loco no. 42881 with much of the side of the Scottish express still attached. The impression is of a giant high-powered tin-opener. (K. & J. Jelley)

40. Settle. And here is the shattering effect it had on one of the coaches. (*Crown copyright*)

under which Waites had had to examine it. The decision to go on to Hellifield was also accepted as being reasonable in view of the time of night, the weather and the exposed location. But knowing that there could be something seriously wrong with his engine, he should have proceeded with extreme caution. Despite his protestations that he had done so, the signal box timings proved conclusively that he had not. The officially estimated speed at the time of the accident was 45 mph. This was considered most excessive in the circumstances and almost certainly accounted for the severity of the disaster. For that reason Driver Waites had to accept some of the blame.

The Settle accident was of a most unusual kind, but not actually the *first* of its kind. In 1915, only three months after Quintinshill, a re-

markably similar accident occurred at Weedon in Northamptonshire. A split-pin fell out of the motion assembly of a George V class 4–4–0 engine which was taking a train from Birmingham to Euston. The cab was hit by flying ballast as the coupling rod came off the crankpin from which the split-pin had fallen. As the rod flayed around in the gap between the tracks until the driver was able to bring the train to a standstill, it hit a sleeper on the down line and displaced the track. Just as at Settle all those years later, ill fate turned what could have been quite a minor mishap into a tragedy, for a train coming the other way reached the scene before any effort could be made to protect the line. At Weedon, though, it was another passenger train – the Irish Mail – and ten people died in it with sixty-four injured. The double-headed fifteen-coach Mail was doing around 70 mph when she hit the damaged track and was instantly derailed. Un-

41. Settle. The displaced right hand motion assembly of Britannia class no. 70052, 'Firth of Tay', seen here at Hellifield depot where the engine was taken for examination after the accident – and where Driver Waites had been hoping to take it before it happened. (*Crown copyright*)

like Settle, all the death and the damage, apart from windows broken by flying ballast, was confined to the innocent passing train for it did not collide with the train that had caused all the trouble. That was left standing safely a little way up from the scene. In all other essential respects it was a strikingly similar occurrence and the cause was the same – careless maintenance. The driver had noticed the split-pin was actually missing whilst waiting at Rugby and had had another fitted, but the fitter did not open the ends properly. On such apparently trivial factors do lives so often depend.

Breakdowns due to poor maintenance or faulty parts have always been a problem on the railways, but remarkably few of such failures lead to disaster. Overall in fact, despite the impression one may have after reading a book devoted to accidents, the safety record of our railways is very high and there are few safer places to be, in this hazardous world, than on a British train.

The Settle incident may have had a precedent in Weedon, but in one sense at least it was unique: it was the last significant accident involving steam trains in Great Britain. The age of steam was finally coming to a close.

94

Index